The

GROSSEST

JOKE BOOK
EVER WRITTEN...

ONLY GROSSER!

LOOKING FOR MORE JOKES TO IMPRESS YOUR FRIENDS AND BUILD YOUR ULTIMATE JOKEMASTER COLLECTION?

YOU'LL LOVE...

THE JOKIEST JOKING JOKE BOOK
EVER WRITTEN . . . NO JOKE!

THE JOKIEST JOKING KNOCK-KNOCK JOKE BOOK
EVER WRITTEN . . . NO JOKE!

THE JOKIEST JOKING TRIVIA BOOK
EVER WRITTEN . . . NO JOKE!

THE JOKIEST JOKING BATHROOM JOKE BOOK
EVER WRITTEN . . . NO JOKE!

THE JOKIEST JOKING PUNS BOOK
EVER WRITTEN . . . NO JOKE!

THE JOKIEST JOKING SPOOKY JOKE BOOK
EVER WRITTEN . . . NO JOKE!

THE JOKIEST JOKING CHRISTMAS JOKE BOOK
EVER WRITTEN . . . NO JOKE!

The

GROSSEST

JOKE BOOK EVER WRITTEN...

ONLY GROSSER!

1,000 JOKES THAT ARE SOOOOO GROSS

Jokes by **BRIAN BOONE**

Illustrations by **AMANDA BRACK**

CASTLE POINT BOOKS
NEW YORK

www.castlepointbooks.com

The Castle Point Books trademark is owned
by Castle Point Publishing, LLC.
Castle Point books are published and distributed
by St. Martin's Publishing Group.

ISBN 978-1-250-32408-5 (trade paperback)
ISBN 978-1-250-32409-2 (ebook)

Design by Noora Cox
Illustrations by Amanda Brack
Images used under license by Shutterstock.com

Our books may be purchased in bulk for promotional,
educational, or business use. Please contact your local
bookseller or the Macmillan Corporate and Premium Sales
Department at 1-800-221-7945, extension 5442, or by
email at MacmillanSpecialMarkets@macmillan.com.

First Edition: 2024

10 9 8 7 6 5 4 3 2 1

Why was the
nose tired?
It was
running
all day.

CONTENTS

INTRODUCING...

THE HUMAN BODY IS NOTHING SHORT OF MARVELOUS.

Amazing, natural, and complex machines, our bodies serve us as we go about our days. Somewhat less fascinating than how everything fits and works together so well is the maintenance of that body. Every single person—even a kid—generates different kinds of waste, and a lot of it. Let's be honest, it's just plain weird that all of us are also disgusting factories that make poop, pee, boogers, fart, puke, and burps, both inside and outside of the bathroom. (And so, for that matter, are animals.)

It's no laughing matter. . . or is it? Of course, it is! As odd as it is how gross we are, it's also hilarious! That's why we made *The Grossest Joke Book Ever Written. . . Only Grosser!* How gross is it, though? It's grosser than gross. This thing is bursting like a pair of pooped-in pants or an overflowing toilet and a torn barf bag with jokes, riddles, goofs, and chunky bits about the things that make us human and the things that make us laugh. That means you're about to read through hundreds upon hundreds of rude and crude wisecracks about stuff that comes out of your mouth, nose, and butt.

The only thing you need is your body—and hopefully you've got a funny bone and a strong stomach. You'll be hurling and tooting with laughter!

BUTT SERIOUSLY

Who would someone call if they were farting glitter? A doctor, as soon as possible!

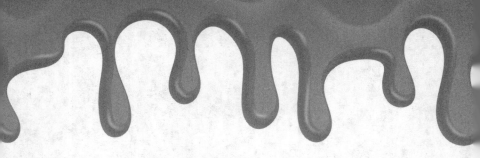

How can you tell if a person has a vivid imagination?
They think that their farts smell good.

What is rude, can travel through solid material, and can bring you to tears?
Farts.

What's worse than trying to spell "hemorrhoids?"
Popping a hemorrhoid.

Knock-knock! *Who's there?*
Pencil. *Pencil who?*
Pencil get stained if you keep letting out those juicy farts!

What cabin at summer camp smells the worst?
Farts & Crafts.

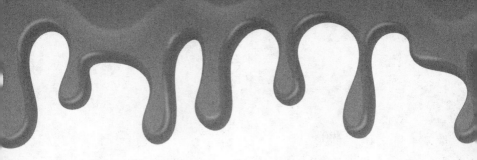

Where does the government keep all of the most valuable farts?
In Fart Knox.

Knock-knock! *Who's there?*
Iva. *Iva who?*
Iva sore butt from that last trip to the bathroom.

What do stinky kids eat for breakfast?
Pop Farts.

Knock-knock! *Who's there?*
Aida. *Aida who?*
Aida bunch of beans and now I'm ready to fart!

Which smells worse, a burp or a fart?
It's hard to say, but together, yours could stop a charging horse.

A doctor goes to dinner one night, and a server comes to the table. The server can't stop scratching his butt. The doctor asks, "Do you have hemorrhoids?" The server replies, "We've only got what's on the menu."

What has nine siblings and smells like poop?
A finger!

What do farts and ninjas have in common?
They're both silent but deadly.

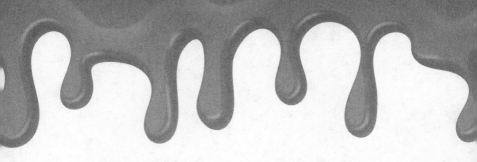

What do a big bowl of chili and a service station have in common?
They'll both give you gas.

What's the worst part about being a cowboy who rides around on a horse every day?
Rawhide.

What do you call a person who is too shy to fart in public?
A private tooter.

What do you call passing gas in a pair of borrowed pants?
A fart transplant!

Why do teenagers fart a lot?
That's the only gas they can afford.

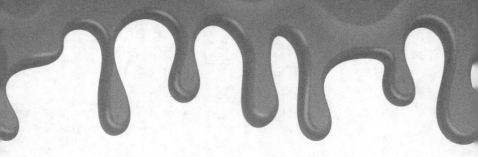

What's the difference between a painting and gas?
One is a work of art, the other is a work of fart.

What do you call a group of superheroes after a chili competition?
The Fart-tastic Four.

What can go right through your pants and never leave a hole?
A fart.

Did you hear about the lost fart? It turned into a burp.

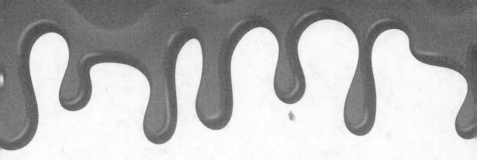

What's yellow, has spiked hair, and smells awful?
Fart Simpson.

What did the poop say to the fart?
"You blow me away!"

Why did the fart have kids?
To raise a stink.

Why didn't the fart finish high school?
It was expelled.

Which kind of fart is the most surprising?
The one with a lump in it.

What's another name for a baby's fart?
A little stinker.

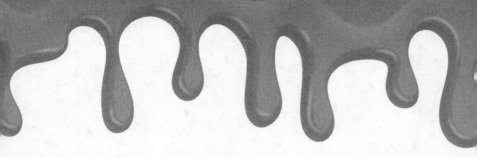

Did you hear about the incident at the bean factory?
There was a gas leak.

A fart is kind of like a speech.
It's not what you say, but rather how you say it.

What's the grossest show on TV?
Fart Tank.

How many farts does it take to clear a room?
Only a phew.

There once was a fart factory that made its own farts and then released them all over town.
Their motto was, "Whoever smelt it, dealt it."

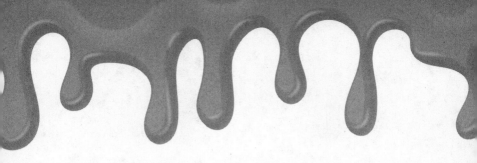

What do you call a Mozart fart?
Classical gas.

Knock-knock! *Who's there?*
Interrupting fart. *Interrupting fart wh—*
Pffffffffffff. . .

In space, no one can hear you fart.
But if you're wearing a spacesuit,
only you can smell it.

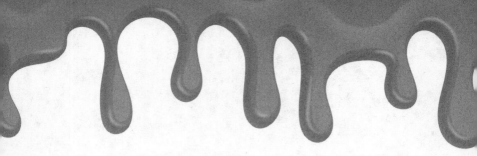

What's the definition of bravery?
Assuming a fart is only going to be a fart one day after a bout with diarrhea.

What's green and smells?
The Incredible Hulk's farts.

Patient: Doctor, I'm here about my hemorrhoids. Do you have any research I can read?
Doctor: Piles!

Patient: Have you been collecting them a while?
Doctor: Yep, I've been sitting on them for a while.

Why do farts smell so bad?
So that the hard-of-hearing can enjoy them, too.

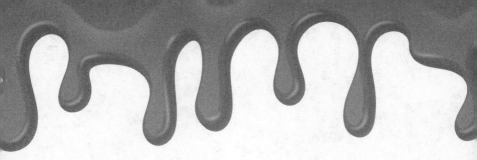

Why do farts smell so bad?
If they didn't, they'd just be called air.

How do you turn a glass of water into seltzer?
Fart into the glass.

I didn't fart.
That was just my insides blowing you a kiss.

Why did the boy fart in the cemetery?
He saw a tombstone that said "RIP."

What did the lady with a run in her stockings do?
She got to a bathroom as quickly as possible.

Why did the woman pass gas in the elevator?
She wanted to take her farting to new levels.

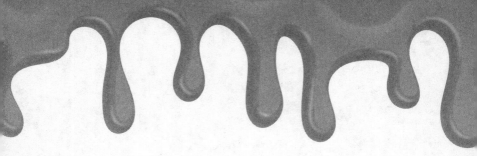

Did you hear about the fart that went on an adventure?
It made a great escape!

Did you hear about the birthday boy who ate too many pieces of prune cake?
He turned his birthday party into a birthday farty.

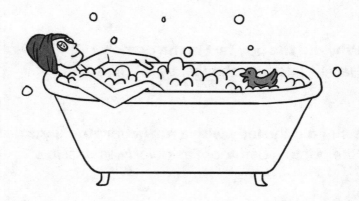

How do you turn a bathtub into a spa?
Eat beans for lunch.

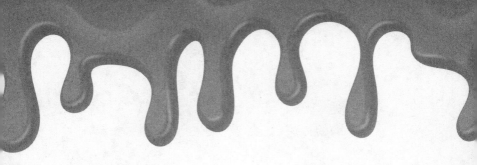

Are farts wholesome?
Sure! Because it's what's on the inside that counts.

What's green and smells like flies?
Kermit the Frog's farts.

What happens when you cross an atomic bomb with beans?
A weapon of gas destruction.

Patient: Doctor, help me. I think I've got hemorrhoids.
Doctor: Swell!

Did you hear about the lackluster student with terrible gas?
He kept getting farter behind, so his parents hired him a tooter.

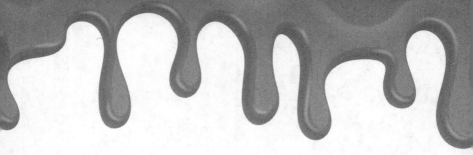

Kid: Mom, I was the only one in class who knew the answer to the question the teacher asked today.
Mom: That's great! What was the question?
Kid: "Who farted?"

Knock-knock! *Who's there?*
Pooh. *Pooh who?*
Pooh-lease stop farting at the dinner table!

Where do butts buy their groceries?
At Hole Foods.

What's worse than smelling a fart?
Tasting one.

What do you call an old butt that has seen it all?
A wise crack.

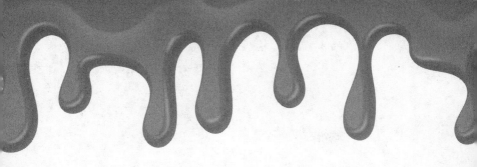

Patient: Doctor, these anti-fart pills don't help at all!
Doctor: Which end did you put them in?

Why are only the cleanest butts allowed to sing solos?
Because they're the soap-ranos.

How can you turn farts into money?
Put them under your pillow for the Toots Fairy.

An old woman went to the doctor's office. "Doctor, I have a farting problem. I fart, but they're silent and don't smell. Help me!" The doctor said, "Take one of these pills every morning." The next week, the patient returned. "Doctor, now my farts smell terrible. What did you give me?"
The doctor replied, "Now that your sinuses are clear, let's work on your hearing."

What do butts and lasers both do?
They both go "pew-pew!"

What do butts eat at the movies?
Poop-corn.

Why are farts worse than bad breath?
Because you can't put a mint in your butt.

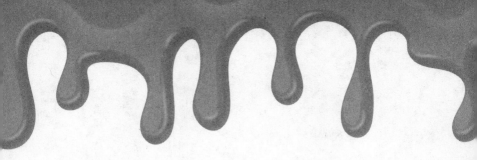

What did one buttock say to the other?
"Between you and me, something smells."

What's worse than sneaking out a fart?
When it turns out to be something more than a fart.

Kid #1: My brother says he farts all day long.
Kid #2: It sounds like he's full of hot air.

Where's the best place to buy beans?
At the gas station.

Which singer smells the worst?
Dolly Fartin'.

How do you take a stinky nap?
Sleep on a hemorrhoid pillow.

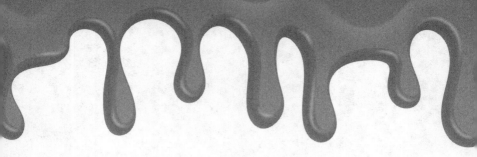

I was having a conversation until my sister came over and farted.
I hate it when she butts in!

What's the worst part about working at a gas station?
Smelling all the burps and farts.

Why did the toilet paper get fired?
He just couldn't crack it.

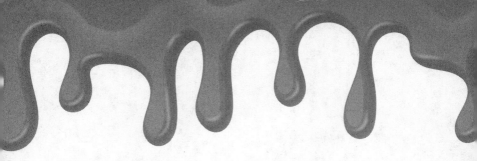

A fart is just a secret your butt whispers to your underwear, and you overheard it.

Want to hear another hemorrhoid joke?
We've got piles!

The thing about hemorrhoids is that they're a real pain in the rear.

What do you try to leave behind you, but always makes their presence known?
Hemorrhoids.

I accidentally brushed my teeth with hemorrhoid cream.
But at least now my rear end smells like peppermint.

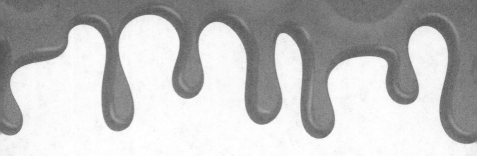

Toothbrush: I have the worst job in the world. Cleaning a stinky, foul mouth? Gross!
Toilet paper: You've got it good, buddy.

I farted on my wallet today.
At least now I have gas money.

Why should you never fart while wearing a grass skirt? It could catch on fire.

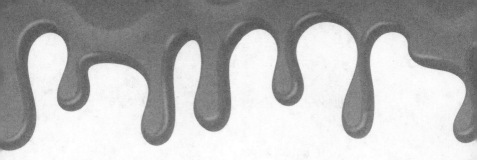

Why did the kid get in trouble twice in school?
First he couldn't hold in his fart, and then he couldn't hold in his laughter over the fart.

Knock-knock! *Who's there?*
Howie. *Howie who?*
Howie going to fart without anyone noticing?

Patient: Doctor, help me, there's something wrong with my butt.
Doctor: Oh my, there's a big crack down the middle!

Patient: Doctor, I have a berry stuck to my butt!
Doctor: I have a cream for that.

How did the butt know it was winter?
Its cheeks were rosy.

Why did everything smell bad to the snowman?
Its butt-on nose.

What day is the biggest day for farting?
Toots-day.

Why do ducks have tail feathers?
To cover up their quacks.

How is your dad like Jupiter?
They're both gas giants.

Is Uranus a gas giant?
Yep, and so is the planet.

Whose tomb smelled like farts?
King Toot.

What happens if you go to bed with an itchy butt?
You wake up with a smelly finger.

What pain in the rear do snowmen get?
Polaroids.

What stinks and looks like a rainbow?
A unicorn fart.

What's the stinkiest piece of clothing? A windbreaker.

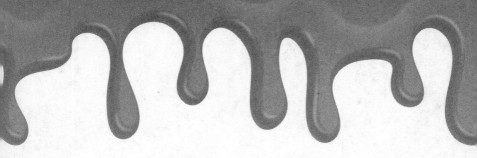

What's invisible and smells like a fart?
Another fart.

What lives in the sky and looks like a butt?
The moon!

Why don't Apple users fart at home?
They don't have Windows.

How can you tell when a moth farts?
They'll suddenly fly straight.

The other day I got flatulence and hemorrhoids.
It was the first time I ever won a game of Scrabble.

What do you call an X-ray of a hemorrhoid?
A polaroid.

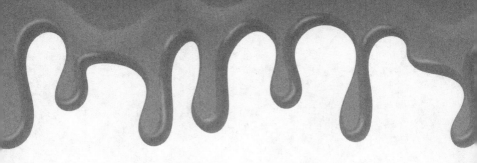

My doctor gave me something he said would treat my hemorrhoids.
But I'm not so sure they deserve a treat.

Did you hear about the hemorrhoid curing seminar?
It was standing room only.

What's the worst tasting doughnut in the world?
A hemorrhoid cream doughnut.

Three people opened up businesses on the same street. The first repaired watches, so he hung a picture of a clock in the window. The second was a baker, and she hung up a picture of a loaf of bread. The third was a doctor who specialized in hemorrhoids. To let people know he dealt with pains in the butt, he hung up a photo of his teenage son.

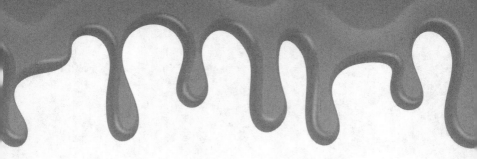

What did the audience do when the comedian bent over?
It cracked up.

Smile and the world smiles with you.
But if you fart, the world suddenly stops smiling.

Why did the mascot pass out?
He farted inside the suit.

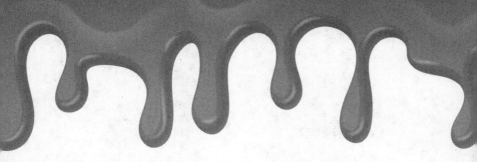

How do runners go faster?
They fart!

How is a fart like an air-raid siren?
It warns others when a bomb is about to drop.

Why do astronauts like space?
In space, no one can hear you fart.

What's the worst part of being Santa's reindeer?
Santa's milk farts.

What's the worst part of being Santa?
Standing downwind behind nine farting reindeer.

Why do butts fart?
Because they can't talk.

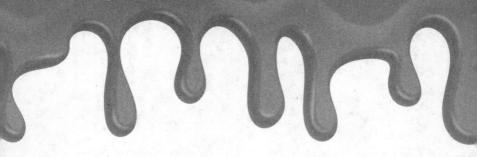

A fart walked into a restaurant.
"You can come in," the manager said. "But don't make a stink."

Two couples are talking at a party. One of the men farted. "How dare you fart in front of my wife!" the other man said. "Oh, I'm sorry," the farter said, "I didn't know it was her turn."

On video calls they have a mute button.
But it should be called a toot button.

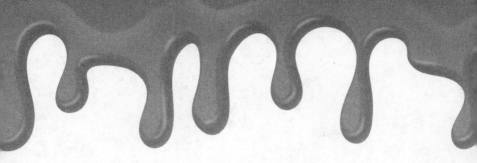

Add to your reading list:
The Heartbreak of Rear-End Odor,
by Maya Buttreeks.

What do your dad and a deli worker have in common?
They both cut the cheese all day.

What's the best way to send a fart to a friend?
Air mail.

What's the sharpest thing in the world?
A fart. It goes straight through your pants.

Why did the kid fart along with the song?
She didn't know the words.

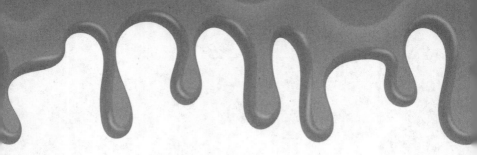

What soda do butts like best?
Squirt.

What do butts eat during movies?
Polyp-corn.

What did one fart say to the other?
"Hey, let's go out tonight!"

What's something you should never pull with your dad?
His finger.

What kind of hemorrhoids do sheep get?
Oh, baaaaaad ones.

"It smells like farts in here," breathed Tom airily.

What numbs a butt?
Anus-thetic.

Another reading list addition:
Gigantic Rear Ends *by Maya Normusbutt.*

Why didn't the hemorrhoid talk to the butt anymore?
They had a falling out.

What did the nudist say when she found an armpit hair in her margarine?
"I can't believe it's not butt hair!"

A man was diagnosed with hemorrhoids, and he got so upset he flipped over the exam table.
That's what we call "roid rage."

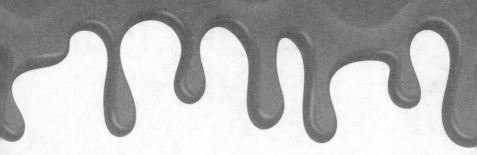

Did you hear about the seminar on how to cure hemorrhoids?
They gave the doctor a standing ovation!

Want to hear a fart joke?
It really rips!

What's gross?
Farting in the bathtub.

What's grosser than that?
Trying to catch the bubbles with your teeth.

Can you use farts to defend yourself?
Sure, if you're familiar with the ancient discipline of fartial arts!

What do you call it when you smell a fart that reminds you of a fart you swear you farted before?
Deja phew!

What's the definition of butting into a conversation?
Farting!

Why do butts fart?
Because otherwise they'd just spew garbage.

I had amnesia and then I farted.
And then it all came back to me.

What do you get if you fart onto a birthday cake?
Not invited back next year.

Two old women are sitting on a bench waiting for a bus. "I've been sitting here for so long, my butt fell asleep," one of them said. The other woman said, "I know! I heard it snoring!"

How can you identify a butt doctor?
He's the guy in the hospital wearing his watch above his elbow.

What do you call someone who blames a fart on a squeaky chair? A liar.

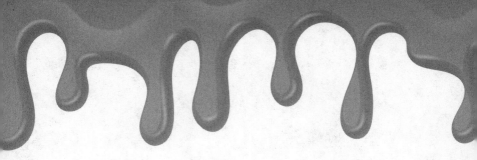

Farting while you're eating is just a "coming attraction."

Is "buttcheeks" one word?
Or should I spread them apart?

How did the pirate captain injure his colon?
He used his hook hand to scratch an itch.

Why do farts make a terrible meal?
They go right through you.

Dentist: How do you clean your top teeth?
Kid: With a toothbrush.
Dentist: And your bottom?
Kid: The same.
Dentist: Ew, use toilet paper!

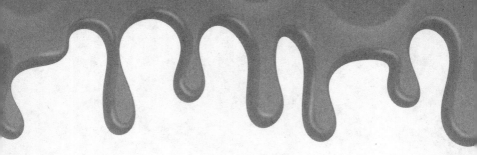

Knock-knock! *Who's there?*
Ivan. *Ivan who?*
Ivan itchy bottom!

Knock-knock! *Who's there?*
Wendy. *Wendy who?*
Wendy you want to pull my finger?

How do you define agony?
Hanging from a ledge and your butt starts to itch.

Another book to read:
How to Be a Proctologist, *by Seymour Butz.*

Why do farts always sound like they're asking a question?
And the answer is usually, "No, now is not a good time to say hello!"

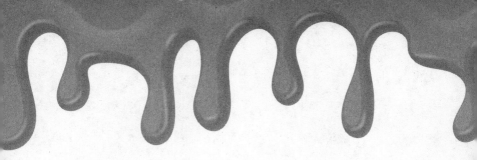

Patient: Doctor! I accidentally got a spoon stuck up there!

Doctor: Relax, and don't make such a stir.

How can you tell if a book was written by a proctologist?

Lots and lots of colons.

Did you see the movie *Intestine*?

It's full of twists!

How was the boy able to fart so loudly that it was heard by 1,000 ears?

He did it in a cornfield.

What did the butt cheeks say after the poop came out?

"It's over between us!"

THE POOP ON POOP

What do you call someone who spends an hour in the bathroom every morning? Dad.

Did you hear about the diarrhea outbreak?
You should have. It's all over town.

Did you hear about the movie *Constipation*?
It was delayed.

What do you call someone using an army latrine?
A pooper trooper.

Why did the piece of poop feel so old?
Because it was turning turdy.

What's the one candy you'd never want to eat?
Reese's Feces.

What did the cannibal do after he broke his fast?
Wiped.

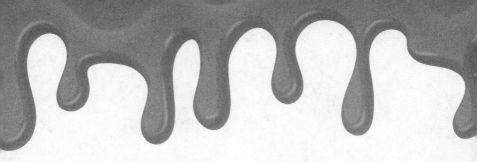

Why do soldiers sit down when they go to the bathroom?
It's the best way to do their doody.

What's the difference between a deep-fried wiener on a stick and a post-cookout poop?
One is a corn dog, and the other is a corned log.

Knock-knock! *Who's there?*
Ike. *Ike who?*
Ike can't help but pee a little bit when I poop.

What did the cowboy have to say about his trip to the bathroom?
He thought it was an okie-dookie.

What do you have after you eat a prune pizza?
Pizzeria!

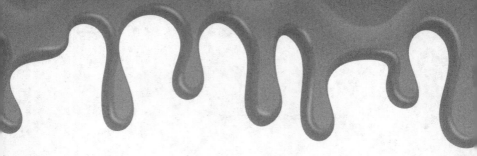

What's the most disgusting kids' book ever written?
Diarrhea of a Wimpy Kid.

Where should you never step on a baseball diamond?
On turd base.

What do toilets order at fast food places?
The number two!

What does Scooby-Doo turn Scooby Snacks into?
Scooby doody doo.

How does poop use the internet?
It logs on.

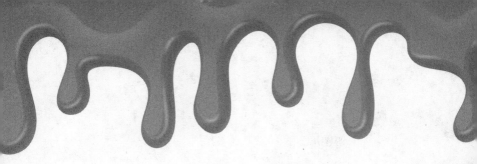

Did you hear about the guy who pooped in his sleep?
He'd taken too many Tylenol BMs.

Why was the security guard standing on dog poop?
She was on doody.

Why did Beethoven go to the bathroom in the woods?
Because he wanted his poop to decompose.

I tried to follow Constipation on Twitter.
But I got blocked.

What's the grossest kind of jazz music?
Scat.

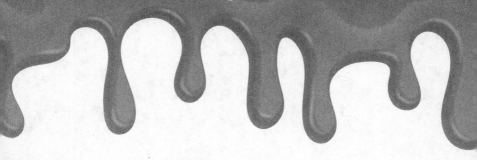

What did food poisoning do to the man's bowels?
It rectum.

What do you call a telephone company worker who took too many laxatives?
A smooth operator.

Knock-knock! *Who's there?*
Noah. *Noah who?*
Noah where the bathroom is? I'm about to blow!

What's the worst air freshener to use in the bathroom?
Poo-poo-ri!

What happens when you put poop on a stick?
You get shish-ka-plops.

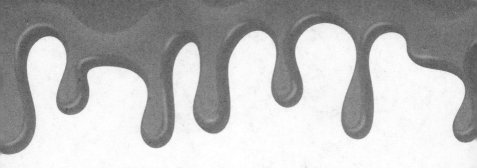

What is grosser than a number two after a lunch of all-you-can-eat buffalo wings?
Not much!

Why did the cowboy have to poop standing up?
Because a cowboy shouldn't squat with their spurs on.

What's brown, smells horrible, and got on all the king's horses and all the king's men? Humpty's dump.

A little boy in church needed to go to the bathroom. "Mom, can I go take a dump?" he asked. "Yes," his mother replied, "but we're in church. Next time don't say 'dump,' say 'whisper.' It's more polite." The next Sunday, the boy is sitting by his father, and again he needed to use the bathroom. "Dad, I have to whisper," the boy said. *"Okay," the father replied. "Whisper in my ear."*

Knock-knock! *Who's there?*
Butternut. *Butternut who?*
Butternut sit in that steaming pile of diarrhea over there.

What do you call a runner with food poisoning?
A salad shooter.

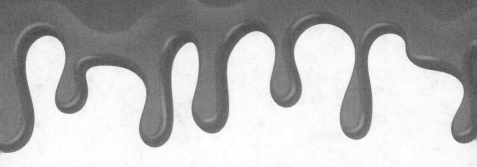

Did you hear about the author who couldn't poop for a week?
Talk about a bad case of writer's block.

What should you never order in a French restaurant?
The poofflé.

Did you hear about the jogger desperately in search of a bathroom? She had the runs.

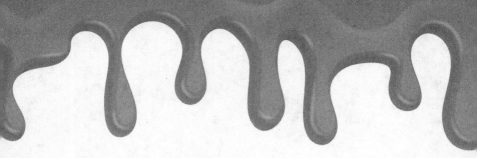

Knock-knock! *Who's there?*
Noah. *Noah who?*
Noah any good laxatives?

Who says, "Tee-hee!" when you poke him in the stomach before they make a huge mess?
Poopin' Fresh.

When you use a toilet on the airplane, where does the poop go?
Nowhere—they never clean those things.

What should you do if you find blue poop in the toilet?
Try to cheer it up.

Why did the turd never get anything done?
Because it was pooped!

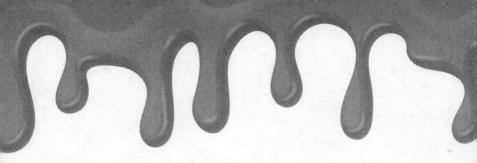

How can you distinguish your dad's poop from others?
It's really corny.

Knock-knock! *Who's there?*
Juicy. *Juicy who?*
Juicy a plunger anywhere around here?

What do you call a kid with a bad case of the runs?
Down in the dumps.

What day of the week should you never use a public restroom?
Splatterday.

Why did the kid poop in the vanilla ice cream?
He wanted a chocolate vanilla swirl.

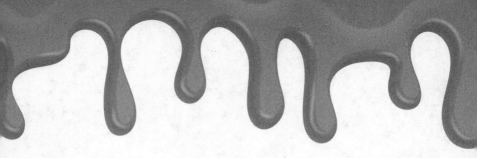

What did the guy get when he couldn't make it to the bathroom in time?
Heavy pants.

Knock-knock! *Who's there?*
Esther. *Esther who?*
Esther a doctor in the house? My diarrhea is out of control!

Knock-knock! *Who's there?*
Europe. *Europe who?*
No, you're a poo!

What basketball team can't control its bowels?
The San Antonio Spurts.

How many logs can you fit in an empty toilet?
One. After that, it's no longer empty.

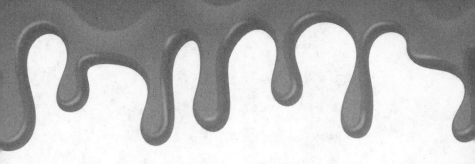

What's the worst thing you can do in the laundry room?
Mistake the dryer for a toilet.

Knock-knock! *Who's there?*
Mop. *Mop who?*
It stinks, doesn't it?

What do
baby mailmen
deliver?
Parcels that
are packed
and loaded.

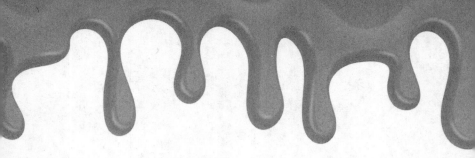

What's worse than finding a fly in your soup?
Finding a fly in your poop.

Patient: Doctor, I need a medication for constipation.
Doctor: This is the #1 doctor-recommended laxative.
Patient: That's great, but I'd prefer the #2.

Do your grandparents have to wear disposable underwear?
Depends.

When is laughter the worst medicine?
It doesn't do much for diarrhea.

What happens after you eat too many Oreos?
A cookie dookie.

Where is the most painful place to go #2 on a car trip?
A fork in the road.

What do you get after eating too many blueberries?
Smurf poop.

What happens after you eat too much alphabet soup?
You get a really bad vowel movement.

What's brown, sticky, and sounds like a clock tower?
Dung.

What do you get when you freeze your poop?
A plop-sicle!

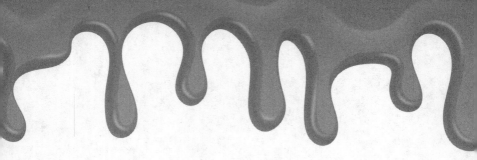

Knock-knock! *Who's there?*
Jamaica. *Jamaica who?*
Jamaica mess in my bathroom?

What's worse than a big juicy fart coming out of your butt?
A big juicy fart going into your butt.

What do you call poop that takes a long and slow time to come out?
A turdle.

Knock-knock! *Who's there?*
A pile up. *A pile up who?*
You better flush!

How is a butt like the Liberty Bell?
They both have a crack.

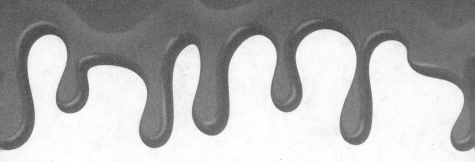

What was the constipated librarian doing in the bathroom?
Working on the backlog.

What did the comedian say when he looked at his poop?
"Yuk-yuk!"

Why did the cook wipe his butt before he pooped?
He liked to make things from scratch.

What place did the piece of poop get in the race?
Turd place.

It's not an uncontrolled turd forcing its way out.
It's just poop popping by to say hello!

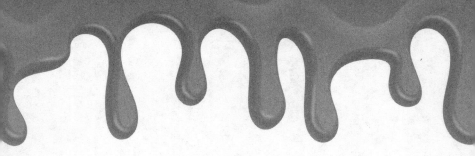

What did the kid say after he made a square poop?
"Ow!"

Patient: Doctor! I have a problem!
Every morning, I poop at 7 on the nose!
Doctor: How is that a problem?
Patient: I don't wake up until 8!

What's the quickest way to lose a couple of pounds?
Drop off a deuce in the bathroom.

Why did the man poop on his lawn?
He was too cheap to buy fertilizer.

What's a good name for a poop that floats?
Bob.

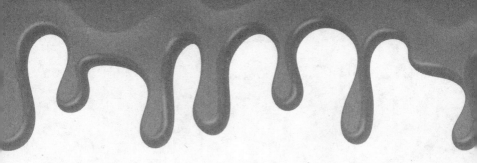

Why did the salesman poop in the furniture store?
Because the customer asked to see a stool sample.

Did you hear about the new album by the band Diarrhea?
It leaked early.

What happens if you eat too many novelty jumping beans?
Your poop will hop right out of the toilet.

What's another name for your dad's turds?
Pop's plops.

What's another name for your mother's poops?
Mom's bombs.

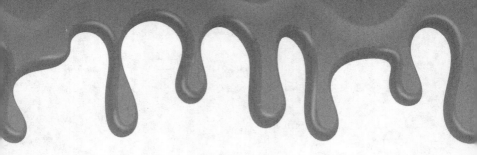

What's weirder than accidentally pooping your pants?
Pooping your pants on purpose.

On which carnival ride is it okay to poop your pants?
The dumper cars.

What's brown, stinky, and spins?
A hula poop.

Did you hear about the guy who wrote something on the internet every time he pooped?
He had a log blog.

What did the worried person leave in the toilet?
A nervous wreck.

Knock-knock! *Who's there?*
Chuck. *Chuck who?*
Chuck your underwear—that fart went rogue.

I was constipated for three months and then it all came out at once.
Talk about a blast from the past.

What do
you call a
model with
diarrhea?
A hot mess.

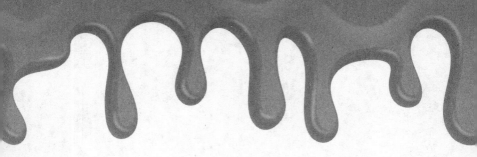

Did you hear about the basketball player who had diarrhea?
He fouled out for double-dribbling.

Did you hear about the constipated engineer?
It's fine now, he worked it out with a pencil.

Kid #1: Did you have corn for lunch?
Kid #2: How did you know?
Kid #1: You forgot to flush.

What's green, hairy, and smells horrible?
I don't know, but somebody left it in the toilet.

Did you hear about the guy who desperately stumbled into the bathroom in the middle of the night and couldn't find the toilet?
It was a fart in the dark.

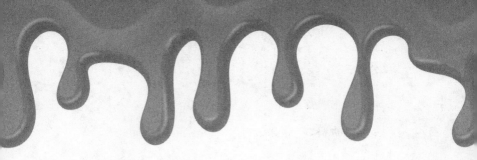

How is your little sibling like a diaper?
They're always full of it and they smell.

Why did the dad only change his baby's diaper one time?
The box said it could hold up to 20 pounds.

What's worse than finding fake poop in your bed?
Finding real poop in your bed.

What's the size of two houses and is full of poop?
A doo-plex.

What's not really any better when it's under control as opposed to when it isn't?
Diarrhea.

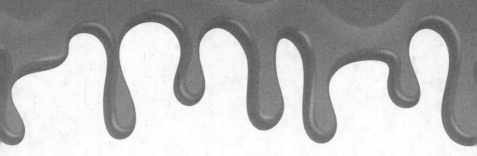

Knock-knock! *Who's there?*
Ooze. *Ooze who?*
Ooze going to clean this toilet?

What did the lifeguard say after he went to the bathroom?
"Everybody out of the pool!"

Did you hear about the movie about an impacted colon?
There was a twist at the end.

What's the smelliest palindrome?
POOP.

How do you know the diarrhea is especially bad?
When you can feel it on the back of your legs.

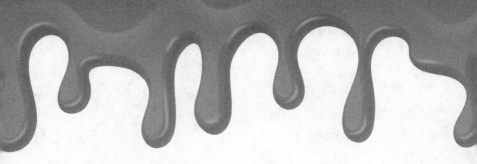

How do butts cool off on a hot day?
With a bottle of Mountain Doo-Doo.

What's the best music to listen to while pooping?
Plop music.

What's made of poop and sits on top of your head?
A hair doo.

When is an American also Russian?
When they've got diarrhea and need a bathroom quickly.

What happens if you eat too much corn?
You get cornstipated.

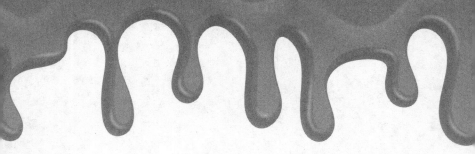

Kid #1: Which hand do you use to clean the toilet?
Kid #2: My right hand.
Kid #1: I'd rather use a brush.

"I didn't make it to the bathroom in time," Tom burst.

"I'm having some pretty bad diarrhea today," Sarah gushed.

"I pooped so hard I think my colon fell out!" said Amanda, feeling disorganized.

What do a volcano, you after eating a hundred hot wings, and a huge bowl of chili have in common?
Everything.

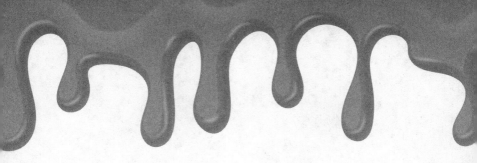

Next week is Diarrhea Awareness Week. It runs until Friday.

What do you call a fart with ambition?
Poop.

What do you get when you're in the middle of nowhere, miles away from a toilet?
Diarrhea.

Knock-knock! *Who's there?*
Smellma. *Smellma who?*
Smellma poo!

My mom got so mad at me for relieving myself in the shower.
I don't know why she's so angry. I mashed it down with my feet.

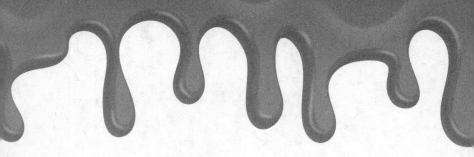

I always need to poop first thing in the morning.
Like, at the crack of dawn!

Who can poop and then make it disappear?
Poo-dini!

The composer was so constipated he died.
He had trouble completing his final movement.

What did the first mate find in the bathroom?
The captain's log.

Did you know diarrhea is hereditary?
It runs in your jeans.

What's brown and smells like poo?
Poo!

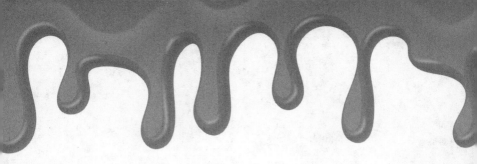

Knock-knock! *Who's there?*
Norma Lee. *Norma Lee who?*
Norma Lee I don't leave such a mess in the bathroom, I'm sorry.

What arrives before the sunrise and smells horrible?
Morning doo-doo.

Four out of five people will suffer from diarrhea.
Which means the fifth person enjoys it.

What's the difference between a fart and poop?
Uh, you don't know?

Who's the stinkiest muppet on Sesame Street?
Dookie Monster.

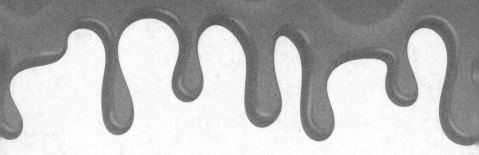

Why did the ballerina walk funny?
Because she made a poo-poo in her tutu.

What smells bad forwards and backwards?
POOP.

What do you call it when a piece of poo comes at you in the ocean?
A fart attack!

A man accidentally pooped in church last week, and everyone moved away from him.
He had to sit on his own pew.

What does a mathematician do after eating a huge dessert?
They make a pie fart.

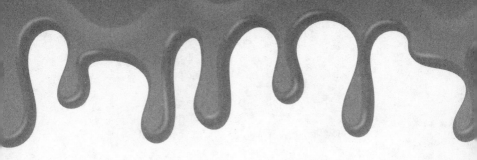

What's a better name for a diaper?
A fanny pack.

What do you call it when you go to the bathroom during dinner?
Making room.

Do you know what kind of
pencil the engineer used?
A no. 2 pencil.

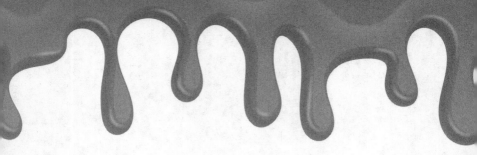

Did you hear about the surfer pooping contest?
It ended in a wipeout.

What kind of pants can you poop in?
Dungarees.

What does Santa poop?
Yule logs.

How is pooping like an infomercial?
Because it's always, "But wait, there's more!"

What do you call a 12-inch turd?
A footstool.

What do surfers wipe themselves with?
Sandpaper.

Knock-knock! *Who's there?*
Eatmop. *Eatmop who?*
I won't do that, that's gross!

Doctor: You have acute diarrhea.
Patient: Ah, thank you!

What's brown and lives in the forest?
Winnie the Poo.

Knock-knock! *Who's there?*
Drew Pealog. *Drew Pealog who?*
Drew Pealog? Sounds like you need more fiber in your diet.

Knock-knock! *Who's there?*
Megan. *Megan who?*
Megan logs in the toilet!

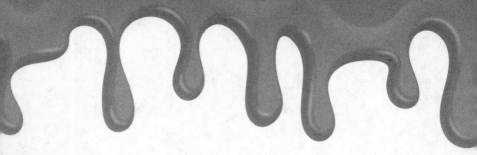

What's worse than putting on your pants?
"Pudding" in your pants.

When should you use shampoo?
When real poo isn't available.

"Things are looking normal since I took that diarrhea medicine," Chris affirmed.

"Sitting on the toilet for an hour and not pooping is fine," said Mandy anticlimactically.

"My turd weighs one-sixteenth of a pound," Brad announced.

"I was in the bathroom for so long," Larry worked out.

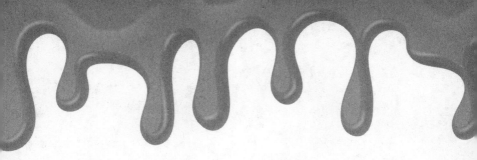

How do you make a 12-inch turd?
Eat a foot-long sandwich.

This year, my New Year's resolution is to poop myself every day.
I hope I can keep the streak going.

Did you hear about the pop star who pooped her pants on stage?
She went right to the top of the farts!

Mommy Diarrhea tried to punish Kid Diarrhea but the punishment never stuck.
She just wasn't very firm.

What do you call it when a leprechaun poops in their tiny green pants?
A lucky streak.

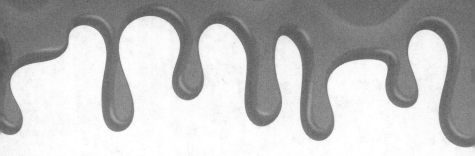

What did the pee say when it beat the poop to the toilet?
"I'm #1! I'm #1!"

Another interesting new book:
My Struggles with Diarrhea, *by Lee Kebum.*

Diarrhea is just your butt's imitation of a sneeze.

What kind of exercise is perfect for people who poop too much? Squats!

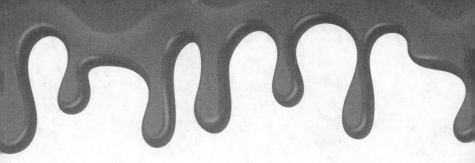

What did Abraham Lincoln make at the White House?
Lincoln Logs.

How do you scare a poop from coming out?
Shout "Scat!" at it.

What's another name for a baby's poop?
A dumpling.

Why did the baker's hands stink?
She kneaded a poo.

A little boy excitedly opened his Christmas present. He was upset when he realized it was just a box full of poop.
"No, Dad," the boy said. "I said I wanted a puppy."

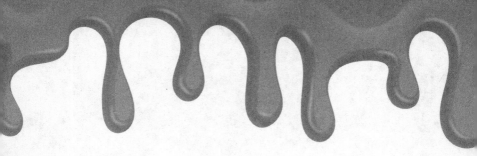

What do you call pooping first thing in the morning?
An AM BM.

What do you call pooping after lunch?
A PM BM.

Why did they fire the train conductor?
She made a poo-poo in her choo-choo.

What happens to diarrhea if it moves through a bunch of butt hair?
It turns into filtered drinking water.

Patient: Doctor, help me. I eat apples, I see apples in the toilet later. I eat bananas, and nothing but bananas come out.
Doctor: Have you tried eating poop?

One more new book to enjoy:
My Life as an Aggressive Turd,
by Heywood Yapinchme.

What's the difference between an oral thermometer and a rectal thermometer?
The taste.

Why are little brothers like laxatives?
They both irritate the poop out of you.

What do you call it when someone texts you to let you know that they're pooping?
Push notifications.

Patient: Doctor, I've got a case of diarrhea.
Doctor: Gross! Take it out of the case and put it in the toilet.

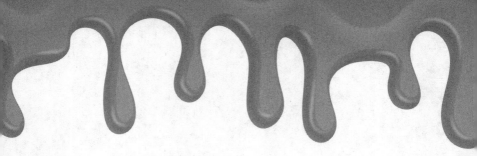

What is a constipated gambler's favorite game?
Craps.

What happens when you eat tainted dynamite?
You get explosive diarrhea.

What would your poop look like if you ate a box of crayons?
It would still be brown. That's just how poop works.

What do garbage trucks and diapers have in common?
They both hold a smelly load.

Want to hear a joke about poop?
You don't?
It's a waste!

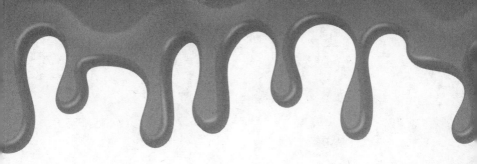

I just pooped my pants.
That's strange. I don't remember eating my pants.

I got thrown out of the Navy.
Apparently "poop deck" is an expression and not an invitation.

How did the guy get poop on his phone?
He was playing Turds with Friends.

Have you played that new game about guiding a turd into the toilet?
It's called Call of Doody.

I called the Constipation Hotline.
I'm still on hold.

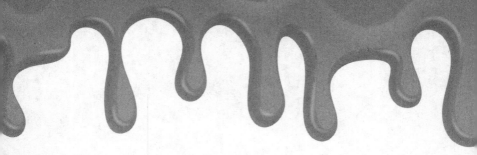

A few more books for you to read:
The Diarrhea Family, *by Manny Luce-Bowles*
Dealing with Constipation, *by U. R. Stuck*
How to Properly Clean Yourself, *by Duke E. Viper*

Two people ran in a race, one with diarrhea.
One ran in short bursts and the other in burst shorts.

Patient: Doctor, I haven't pooped in weeks.
Doctor: Well, don't just sit there.

What did the butt say to the poop?
"Hey, can you do me a solid?"

If pooping is answering the call of nature. . .
Is farting a missed call?

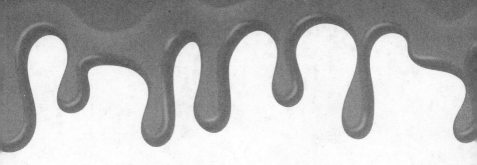

What did the poop say as it exited the rear end?
"It looks like this is the end."

Poop jokes aren't my favorite jokes.
But they're a solid number two!

Why did the kid bring toilet paper to a New Year's Eve party? He was a party pooper.

URINE
TROUBLE

Why do guys
take showers
instead of baths?
Because peeing
in the bathtub
is disgusting.

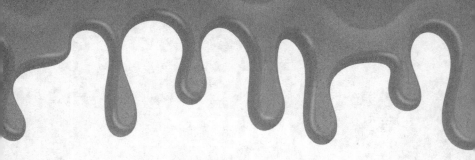

What's another name for the world's biggest toilet?
A swimming pool.

Two boys go into two separate bathroom stalls. They finish up at about the same time. The first boy goes to the sink to wash his hands. The second boy is about to leave, and the first boy asks, "Aren't you going to wash your hands? I was taught to always wash my hands after using the bathroom."
The second boy laughed and said, "Well, I was taught not to pee on my hands."

Did you hear about the guy who went to Costco and then went to the doctor?
First he got free samples, and then he left pee samples.

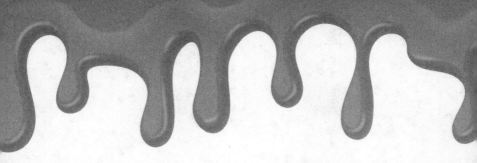

Knock-knock! *Who's there?*
Bean. *Bean who?*
Bean forgetting to put the seat up, haven't you?

What's the worst thing to find in your freezer?
Frozen pees.

What's the difference between apple juice and pee?
A kid will wash their hands if they get covered in apple juice.

What smells like asparagus but tastes way worse than asparagus?
Asparagus pee.

What's thirty feet long and smells like pee?
A line dance at a retirement home.

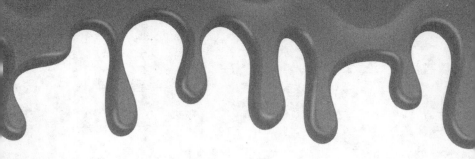

Have you ever heard of a swimming ool?
It's a swimming pool with no P. They're very rare.

What days of the week is your urine stream at its strongest?
Saturdays and Sundays. All the other days are weak days.

What did the dad say to the boy who peed in his garden? "Urine for a punishment!"

Kid: Can I go to the bathroom?
Teacher: Only if you can sing the alphabet.
Kid: ABCDEFGHIJKLMNOQRSTUVWXYZ
Teacher: Where's the "P"?
Boy: Running down my leg!

How do you wash your hands with a urinal?
Just use that soap disc sitting at the bottom.

What's the difference between boiling eggs and pea soup?
Anybody can boil eggs.

Do you want to join the Pee-Pee Club?
Congratulations, urine!

What do they call urinals in Russia?
Yuri-nals.

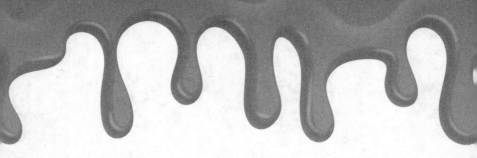

What's the best thing about swimming in the ocean?
Nobody will care if you pee a bit.

Never buy a bag of ice.
They've got free ice in the urinals at most every restaurant in town!

How do you know you've had one too many sodas? When your pee turns fizzy.

What's the worst-tasting cake in the world?
A urinal cake.

Why is sand wet?
Because sea-weed!

Patient: Where's the urology office?
Receptionist: Just follow the yellow brick road.

What are doctors' favorite beverages?
Probably those little cups of urine they always want.

Knock-knock! *Who's there?*
Impatient bladder. *Impatient bladder wh—*
Never mind, it's too late.

Three kids are walking through a forest when they come across a giant slide. A wizard stands beside it all and tells the kids that whatever drink they want will appear on the slide as they go down it. The first kid gets on the slide and shouts, "Root beer!" The second kid goes down the slide and shouts, "Lemonade!"

The third kid hits the slide and shouts, "Weeeeee!"

What's the difference between pineapple and a diaper? One is full of Ps and one is full of pee.

What kind of exercise do you do after having too many Starbucks drinks?
Pee-lattes.

What does the lifeguard say after he goes to the bathroom?
"Everybody out of the pool!"

What do babies and swimming pools have in common?
While they're both full of pee, only one can hold their water.

A man finishes peeing and his wife walks in after him. "Hey," she asks, "did you just pee and not flush?" "Yes," he said. "That's quite clear."

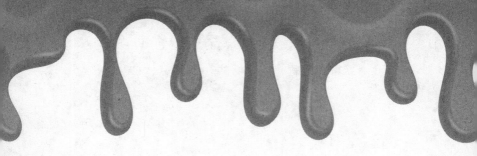

Kid: Dad, I have to pee very badly!
Dad: Son, you're 12 years old. You should be good at that by now.

I just love pee jokes.
They're comedy gold.

How do you make sure you
don't get a baby shower?
Be alert when you change the diaper.

How are friends like snowflakes?
When you pee on them, they disappear forever.

Pee is like your future.
Except that it's clearer.

Teacher: Students, if you need to pee, put your hand up.
Student: I tried that, but it just ran through my fingers.

What do you call a guy who pees green?
A doctor. You call a doctor.

A great new book to read:
The Yellow River, *by I.P. Freely.*

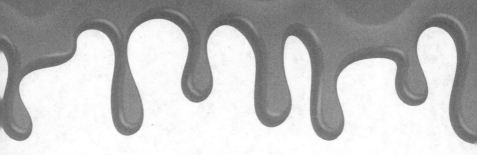

Knock-knock! *Who's there?*
Thumping. *Thumping who?*
Thumping is dribbling down my leg.

How can you tell that Santa and his reindeer visited your house?
There's yellow snow on the roof.

What are
snowflakes
made out of?
Snowman pee.

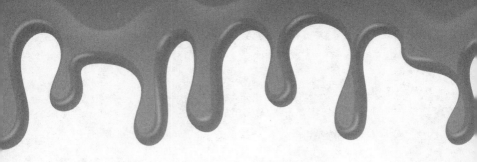

I finally met someone who likes peeing on fruit as much as I do.
Tomorrow, we're going on a date.

There's a lot of things I must do in the morning.
Going to the bathroom is a clear #1.

I took a urine test at the doctor's office today.
I have to stop stealing things.

Last night, my dream came true.
I dreamt I was peeing.

Knock-knock! *Who's there?*
Urine. *Urine who?*
Urine luck! The bathroom's free.

If you think you can safely pee on an electric fence, well then, urine for a shock.

I don't know why people hate kidney stones so much.
They come in pees!

What does the King do after he goes to the bathroom? He makes a royal flush.

Last night, I slept like a baby.
I woke up every two hours to pee.

Knock-knock! *Who's there?*
Tennis. *Tennis who?*
Tennis too many times to go to the bathroom in one day, right?

Want to hear a joke about asparagus pee?
It stinks.

What's worse than peeing the bed at a sleepover?
Peeing in somebody else's bed at the sleepover.

How do you keep your legs warm during the winter?
Just go!

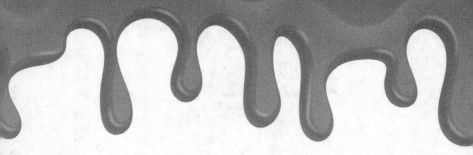

There are two kinds of people in this world: those who pee in the shower.
And liars.

Kid #1: Have you ever been on the TV?
Kid #2: No, but my brother did, and he got in trouble, so I always use the toilet.

Usually nobody notices if you pee a little in the swimming pool.
I got kicked out because I did it from the diving board.

I thought that my parents had installed automatic lights because they come on every time I get up to use the bathroom in the middle of the night.
It turns out I've been peeing in the refrigerator.

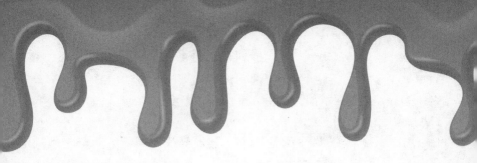

Knock-knock! *Who's there?*
Centipede. *Centipede who?*
Centipede on the Christmas tree because you were naughty.

I remember when I was 10 and wet the bed. My mom got so angry.
When she came in and saw me, she yelled, "Get off the nightstand and stop peeing!"

"I have flow issues," Bruce sputtered.

True happiness is like peeing your pants.
Most people experience both during childhood.

Should you wipe after you pee?
Yes, especially if it's all over the toilet seat.

What should you watch when you need to pee?
Anything streaming.

Knock-knock! *Who's there?*
Pecan. *Pecan who?*
Pecan go right into the toilet.

"I couldn't hold it in any longer!" Evelyn leaked.

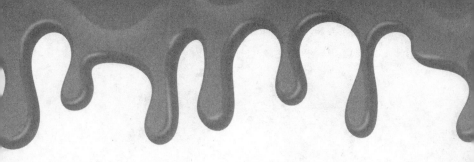

Kid #1: Did you wet your pants in school today?
Kid #2: Yeah, but it was P.E.

A man walked into a restaurant and asked the manager, "Do you have gold toilets? All I remember about last night is that I was here, and I peed in a golden toilet." The manager said, "No, we don't have golden toilets."
Then he picked up the phone and said, "Hey, Billy, we found the guy who peed in your tuba!"

Knock-knock! *Who's there?*
Anita. *Anita who?*
Anita get in there, fast!

Kid #1: Have you ever peed in the shower?
Kid #2: Yes, but it was an accident.
Kid #1: How was it an accident?
Kid #2: I tend to pee a little when I poop.

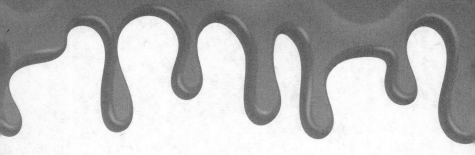

Why did the astronaut pee on the ceiling?
He wanted to go where no one had gone before.

Where did the bee go pee?
At the BP station.

What's the wettest nation on Earth?
Urination.

Why did the kid pee on his algebra book? Because he was a math whiz.

What did Elsa sing while she was in the bathroom?
"Let it flow, let it flow ..."

What did the banker call going to the bathroom?
Checking out their liquid assets.

Knock-knock! *Who's there?*
Don. *Don who?*
Don think you can get away with peeing on the seat again!

What's the difference between
boogers and Brussels sprouts?
No one likes to eat Brussels sprouts.

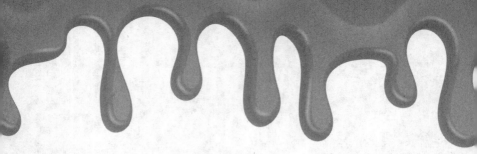

What do you call a wall of boogers?
A picket fence.

Knock-knock! *Who's there?*
Throat. *Throat who?*
**Throat out that sandwich! It's covered
in boogers!**

What's full of boogers and smells?
A nose.

Why did the little boy only eat boogers?
He was a picky eater.

Knock-knock! *Who's there?*
Will. *Will who?*
**Will you get me a tissue? Snot is dripping into
my mouth.**

What do you call a booger that's been on a diet?
Slim pickins.

Why do we have fingernails?
So we can dig deeper!

What restaurant is the critics' pick?
Booger King!

Why don't snowmen eat carrot cake? They're afraid it has boogers in it.

What do ghosts pick from their noses? Boo-gers.

Why is there no such thing as an empty nose?
Because even a clean one has fingerprints.

Did you hear about the snot that got back together with its ex?
It couldn't resist its old phlegm.

What do noses and apple pies have in common with each other?
They're both crusty.

How are boogers and fruits similar?
Both taste best when they're fresh.

What do toenails and old cheese have in common?
Their smell.

What do noses and melted
cheese have in common?
They both smell and get runny.

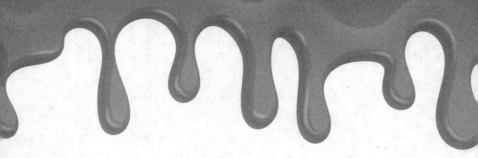

When is a booger not a booger?
When it's snot.

Knock-knock! *Who's there?*
Adam's not. *Adam's not who?*
Adam's not is dripping from Adam's nose.

What do you call wrapping a booger in a tissue?
Saving your dessert.

"Me? A runny nose? Never!" Ginny snorted.

Why did the snot die of old age?
Because slime flies!

What's green, lives in your nose, and dances?
Boogies.

"I still haven't found that booger," said Allen boringly.

A little boy picked his nose and then licked his finger. His father noticed him doing it and said, "Son, stop that! That is absolutely disgusting!" Then he took a tissue and wiped the booger off of his finger. "Hey, I should be the one mad at you," the boy said. "And why is that?" his father asked. "I didn't get to eat it!"

Knock-knock!
Who's there?
Hatch.
Hatch who?
Ew, you just sneezed everywhere!

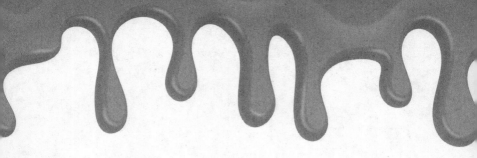

Why didn't the kid eat his boogers?
He was too full from all the boogers he'd eaten already.

What would you find in a fast-food employee's nose?
Cheese boogers.

I tried to take a picture of myself with my finger in my nose.
It came out picks-elated.

What should you do if you see boogers on strike?
Pick it!

What did the nose say to the finger?
"Stop picking on me!"

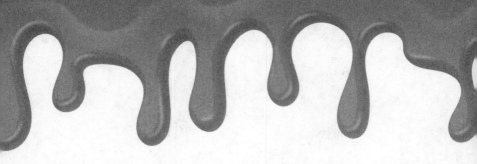

Who's scary and covered in snot?
The Boogeyman.

"Why is my voice so raspy," Hank asked phlegmatically.

What lives in your nose and smells bad?
P.U.-cus.

Why was the nose tired? It was running all day.

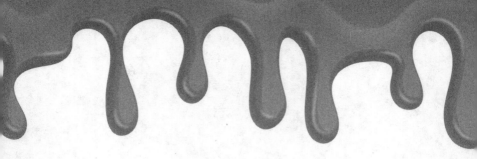

What's yellow and looks like snot?
Snot that got sun bleached.

What's near England and is covered in slime?
Snotland.

What do you call the part of the body that's caked in boogers?
The finger!

What drips out of a cat?
Mew-cus.

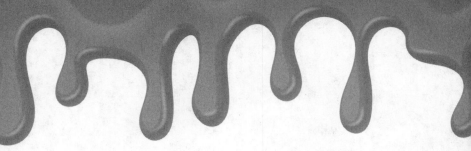

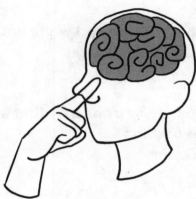

When is it time to stop picking your nose? When you reach the brain.

Why should you never put boogers in your dinner?
Because they taste terrible!

Did you hear about the kid who sneezed while baking a cake?
His nose was full of sugar boogers.

Knock-knock! *Who's there?*
Ollie. *Ollie who?*
Ollie ta booger if you've got one!

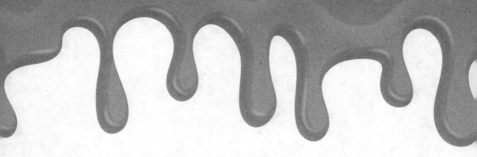

What's green and white and hangs from a tree?
Tarzan's used tissues.

What do you call a fly that's green and doesn't have wings?
A booger.

I'm very full of myself.
But that might be because I've been biting my nails and swallowing my boogers.

How are boogers
like berries?
They're picked
and eaten.

What's the difference between boogers and lima beans?
Kids won't eat lima beans.

Why should you never pick your nose and eat what you find?
Because that finger is probably very dirty.

When is it time to stop picking your nose?
When you go too far and touch something that makes you forget how to pick your nose.

Knock-knock! *Who's there?*
Bogey. *Bogey who?*
Bogey hangin' from your nose!

GAG GAGS

Knock-knock!
Who's there?
Stan.
Stan who?
Stan back.
I'm about to spew!

Where did Marilyn go when she needed to barf?
The hurls room.

Do you want to hear a joke about vomit?
Coming right up!

What's green, weighs 200 tons,
and fills the ocean with puke?
Moby Sick.

How do you make a fresh lunch?
Puke in reverse!

A book you might like to read:
Vomiting Techniques, *by Anya Neeze.*

What happened to the teenager who drank eight lemon-lime sodas?
She threw seven up.

What color is a belch?
Burple.

What drink will always make you burp?
Belch's Grape Juice.

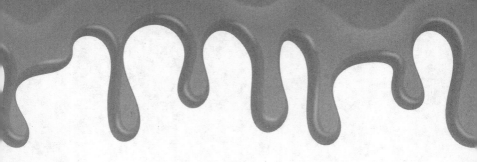

Man: Doctor, help me! Every morning when I wake up and look in the mirror, I throw up. What's wrong with me?
Doctor: I'm not sure, but your eyesight is perfect.

How does a burp cut loose and go wild?
It goes out the other end.

What did the nervous, overfed pitcher do on the mound? He hurled!

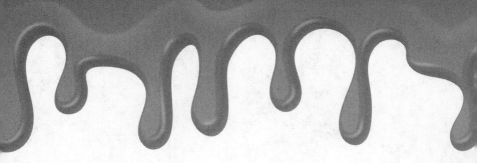

What's soft and warm at bedtime but hard and stiff in the morning?
Vomit.

Did you hear about the guy who missed the puke bucket and vomited all over the floor?
It was beyond the pail!

Did you hear about the pilot who barfed on the plane?
He got through it with flying colors.

What do Italians call vomiting?
Barf-a-roni.

What's the difference between puke and school lunch?
School lunch is served on a tray.

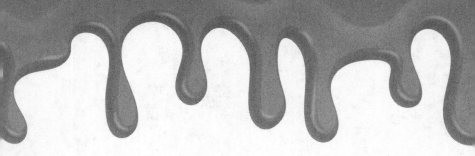

What do dogs call their own vomit?
The soup course.

What did one burp say to another?
"Let's be stinkers and go out the back end!"

On what airline does everyone get sick during the flights?
Spew-nited.

Did you hear about the golfer who was so nervous about the tournament that he vomited? I suppose it's just barf for the course.

What machine plays music so bad
it makes you want to vomit?
A pukebox.

What happened when the kindergartener got sick during finger painting class?
She made a wretch-a-sketch.

Patient: I've been vomiting all day. Can you recommend anything for food poisoning?
Doctor: Sure, raw chicken usually works.

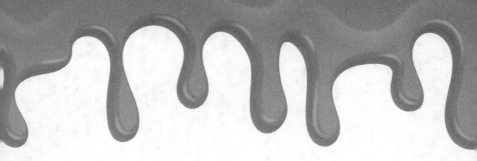

What's a good name for a guy who pukes all the time?
Ralph.

Why did the girl get sick at the haunted house?
It was too spew-ky.

Knock-knock! *Who's there?*
Yule. *Yule who?*
Yule be sorry if you make another trip to the buffet.

How do you make pickles that will make your friends barf?
Start with a puke-cumber.

How can you tell you've got bad breath?
Every time you breathe, a few nose hairs fall out.

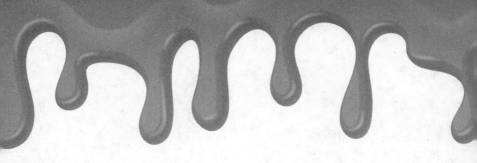

What do you get when you eat a candy bar, throw it up, take it to the beach, and then eat the candy bar again?
A retreat.

What does a bear eat after a teeth cleaning?
The dentist.

What did the waiter say to the toilet?
"One dinner, coming right up!"

Kid #1: Hey can I have a piece of gum? My breath is really bad.

Kid #2: Actually, how about you have some of this toilet paper?

Bad breath is disgusting.

But I don't need to worry about that since discovering all this free gum under my desk.

How do you make someone's bad breath smell like a fart? Ask them to stand on their head.

Did you hear about the dentist who diagnosed his patient's bad breath? The patient was in the waiting room at the time.

My friend's breath is so bad.
His milk farts are a nice relief.

You know your breath is bad if you walk past a clock and it says, "Tic Tac."

Why did the teeth fall out?
The breath was so bad they planned an escape.

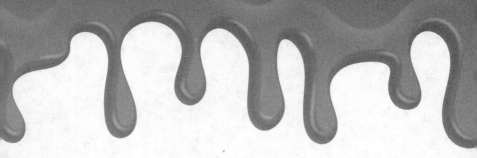

What smells like acid and flies through space?
Halley's Vomit.

The man threw up and lost his lunch.
And then he found it again.

Why did the diner send a plate of vomit back to the kitchen?
The cook wanted feedback.

Why did the cannibal vomit the fireman?
You can't keep a good man down.

How can you eat the exact same meal a second time?
When you throw it up.

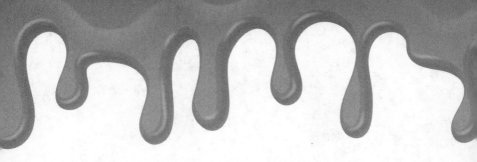

A man went to a restaurant and asked for a bowl of chili. The server said, "Sorry, but that man over there just got the last bowl." The man saw the other diner and noticed that the chili bowl was still full. He sat down and said, "Excuse me, could I buy this chili off you?" The second man said "Sure, go for it." So the man started to eat the chili. As he got down to the bottom, he noticed something unusual. Turning his fork over, he discovered a dead rat in the chili and immediately vomited the chili back into the bowl. The other man leaned over and said, "That's as far as I got, too."

I was going to talk about why I hate to vomit. *But then something suddenly came up.*

Where is the most beautiful place to vomit? *A hot air balloon, although it isn't so beautiful for the people on the ground.*

The King
burped!
And so he
issued a
royal pardon.

What do you get when you sneeze and barf at the same time?
A breeze.

I feel so cheated.
The vomit bag on my flight was empty.

I knew a guy who would go to a fast food place and order two hamburgers, two fish sandwiches, and two chicken sandwiches.
He called it "Noah's Barf."

A lady got into the elevator and started throwing up.
It was gross on so many levels.

What stinks and comes in a bag?
Vomit.

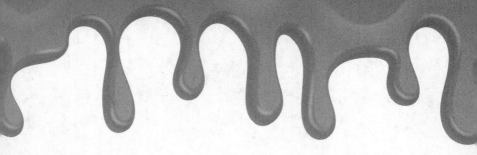

What do you say to vomit that hasn't been cleaned up in a year?
"Happy barf-day!"

What's gross about twins conjoined at the mouth?
When one of them needs to throw up.

My dentist was shocked by
how bad my breath was.
And that was on a Zoom call.

Why did the kid throw up after eating too many German sausages?
It brought out the wurst in him.

Did you hear about the tennis player who went to serve and threw up the ball?
Yeah, I don't know why she ate a tennis ball.

Passenger: Do you have room in the front seat for a pizza?
Driver: Sure.
Passenger throws up in the front seat.

Last night my father told me a bunch of jokes. They were terrible, but on the last one, he threw up, right at the punchline.
It was the sickest joke I've ever heard!

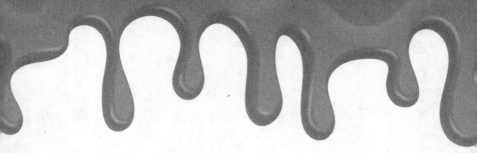

I didn't want to know that she had to vomit.
But some things just come up in conversation.

I threw up so much today.
Which is weird because I don't remember eating any vomit.

What's brown, green, and smells like people?
Cannibal vomit.

What's hairy and smells like vomit?
A mustache.

I went to a party, everyone ate the cake, and then we all threw up.
It wasn't a very happy barf day.

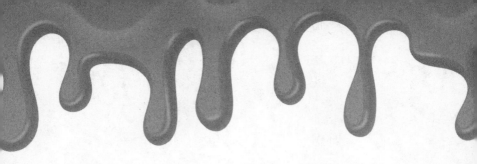

Did you hear about the cannibal with a stomachache?
It must have been someone he ate.

What happened to the man who ate too much blue cheese?
He blue chunks.

What tastes worse than day-old vomit casserole?
Week-old vomit casserole.

Knock-knock! *Who's there?*
Mushroom. *Mushroom who?*
Not mushroom in my stomach, I'm gonna blow chunks!

Knock-knock! *Who's there?*
Fajita. *Fajita who?*
Fajita another bite, I'll hurl!

"I hate how my barf tastes," said Tom acidly.

What's green and has four legs?
Seasick twins.

"These jokes turn my stomach," said Omar wretchedly.

My friend met the love of his life when they were both vomiting over the side of a cruise ship.
It was a match made in heaving!

Who is Puke Skywalker's father?
Barf Vader.

What do a volleyball server and a pregnant woman have in common?
They both throw up a lot.

What's the worst part about being so sick you try to make yourself vomit?
I'm not sure, but I can't put my finger on it.

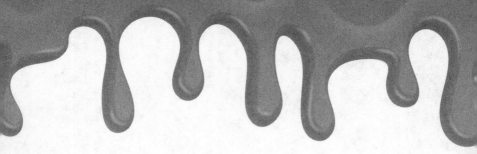

Why did the man throw up after eating a fried-chickpea sandwich?
It made his stomach falafel.

A man walked out of a buffet, and he immediately threw up. He almost got some on the arm of the police officer who was standing on the street, who quickly moved. "Not on my watch!" he said.

What did the frustrated cannibal say?
Nothing. He just threw up his hands.

Patient: Doctor, can you give me anything to help my bad breath?
Doctor: Take a spoon of horse manure twice a day.
Patient: That will cure it?
Doctor: No, but you won't notice the natural smell of your breath anymore.

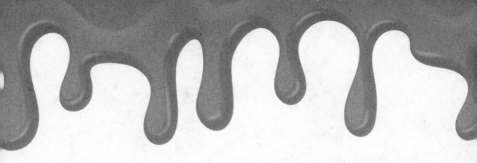

Did you hear about the guy who inhaled his own vomit?
It's so aspirational.

Why did the kid burp and then fart?
He thought the burp seemed lonely.

I threw up a bunch of alphabet soup.
Not only was I sick, but it's then I realized I couldn't read.

Have you read this book?
Making Your Mouth Stink, *by Hal E. Toesis.*

What do you say to your vomiting friend Chuck?
"What's up, Chuck?"

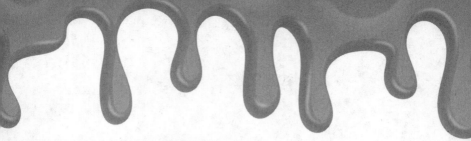

What's food backwards?
Puke.

What's brown and smells like vomit?
Puke.

Doctor: How's that kid who swallowed the half-dollar?
Nurse: No change yet.

What's the best way to lose five pounds in one day?
Food poisoning.

"I am not full of hot air," Lindsay belched.

"Now no one can detect my halitosis," said Eric breathlessly.

A man goes into a public bathroom when he sees another guy sticking a finger down his pants. "I'm doing this to make myself throw up," he says. "How's that going to work?" the other guy asks. The first guy then stuck his finger under his nose.

I'd forgotten about that rancid sandwich I'd eaten earlier. But it's all coming back to me now.

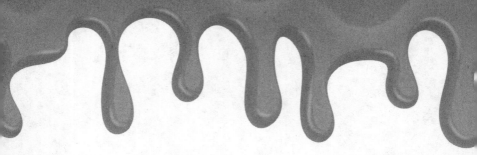

"Honestly, it makes me want to vomit," was Oliver's gut reaction.

Knock-knock! *Who's there?*
Alda. *Alda who?*
Alda potato salad went bad. The bathroom will be toxic!

How do you make a face mask stink?
Breathe into it.

What do burps and kitchens have in common?
Both smell like dinner.

I was having so much fun drinking pop, I belched, "This is a gas!"
Soda speak.

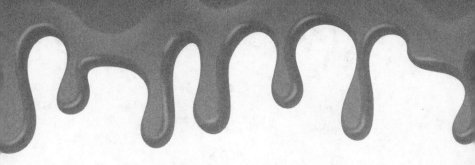

What's the dentist's worst tool?
His finger.

What's the worst thing you can hear a dentist say?
"Are you going to eat that?"

This is the last joke about vomiting.
I promise not to bring that up anymore.

Did you hear about the man who couldn't stop pooping and vomiting at the same time?
It's an extremely sick joke.

PITS, POPS

Which button
stinks most?
A belly button.

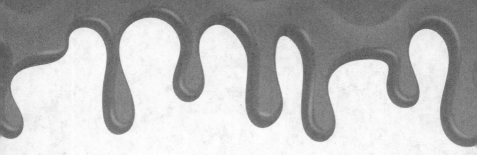

What did the gross magician say when he picked at his wound?
"Scabracadabra!"

What's the stinkiest city?
Pits-burg.

Did you hear about the guy whose armpits were so smelly?
His Speed Stick slowed down.

Why did the booger and the pimple team up?
They got tired of being picked on!

What is dandruff's favorite cereal?
Corn flakes.

Did you hear about the girl with too much earwax?
It was downright ear-ie.

What's the best part about flossing your teeth?
Finding all those snacks for later!

What do zits drink?
Pop!

What do you
call a little zit?
A simple pimple.

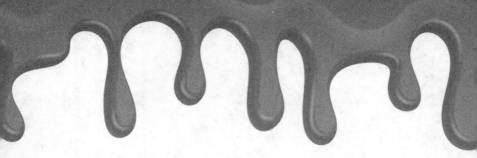

Knock-knock! *Who's there?*
Bella. *Bella who?*
Bella button lint tastes great!

Knock-knock! *Who's there?*
Namir. *Namir who?*
Namir earwax, better eat some belly button lint if you're still hungry!

What do Italian teenagers eat for dinner?
Zit-i.

Why should you not worry when you get a pimple?
Because zits just something that happens.

What's worse than having an ear full of earwax?
Having an ear full of earwigs.

I used to hate the huge zit on my face. But it's growing on me.

Why didn't anyone want to hang out with Dandruff Dave?
He was flaky.

For weeks my dad's arms had been covered with scabs. Then one morning, they were gone! I thought about all this as I ate a bowl of this new red, salty cereal.

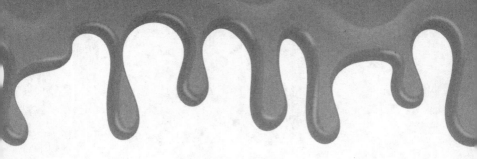

What do you call a guy who makes armpit fart sounds all night?
A pit orchestra musician.

I remember when my ears used to be a lot filthier.
Sorry, I was just waxing nostalgic.

When does it hurt to smile? When you've got pimples in your dimples.

What's the difference between lice and dandruff?
Dandruff has almost no taste at all.

Why did the environmentalist use so much mouthwash?
He wanted to fight air pollution.

How can you tell when a pimple has gotten too big?
It gets its own zit code.

What's covered in zits, carries a sword, and meows?
Pus in Boots

What's the difference between lice and dandruff?
Dandruff has way less protein in it.

How do you make dandruff soup?
From scratch!

What looks like beef jerky, tastes like beef jerky, but isn't beef jerky?
Scabs!

Did you hear about the kid with very stinky armpits? His teacher gave him an A because he didn't raise his hand in class.

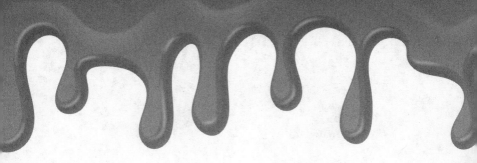

What kind of button makes a finger smell?
A belly button.

Want to hear a joke about feet?
It's pretty corny.

What's crispy and smells like feet?
Bunion rings.

What's full of sailors and smells like sweat?
The Navel Academy.

Seeing acne makes me vomit.
It must be a cyst-emetic reaction.

What's crunchy, red, and melts in your mouth?
A bag of chocolate covered scabs.

How did the kid's mom prevent him from biting his nails?
She made him wear shoes.

Kid #1: Hey, I didn't know you had six toes on each foot.
Kid #2: I don't. That's just fungus that got out of control.

How do you catch dandruff? Shake your head over a paper bag.

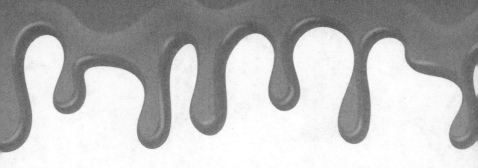

What's the difference between your gym socks and your school lunch? If you get hungry enough, you can eat the socks.

"I want chicken pox!" said Buddy rashly.

Here's another great new book to read:
Manufacturing Armpit Stink, *by Bea O'Problem.*

What smells worse than your feet?
Your best friend's feet.

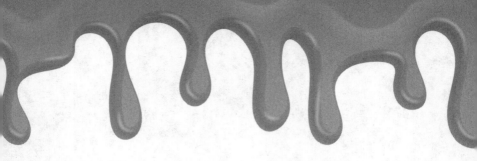

Want to know how someone with foot fungus feels?
Just walk a mile in their shoes.

How is a scab like a potato chip?
Bet you can't eat just one!

What did the pimple say to the butt?
"I'm tired of people picking on us!"

How do you send a pus sample to your doctor?
Use the pus office.

What happened to the eye doctor who fell into the lens maker?
He made a spectacle of himself.

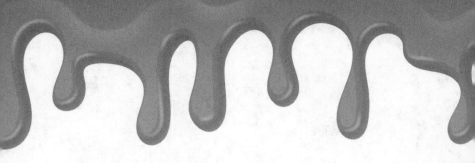

I thought her freckles were adorable.
Until they started to swarm.

What's pink, white, and creamy, but doesn't taste like a strawberry parfait?
Pink eye!

Excuses are like armpits.
Everyone has them, and they all stink.

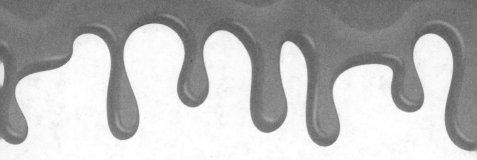

Should you file your nails?
No, you can just throw them away.

What's the difference between toe jam and toe jelly?
It's a preference of chunky vs. smooth.

Why did the Parisian stick his feet in a hot pot full of cheese?
He wanted to make French bunion soup.

What's got art on the ceiling and pus everywhere else?
The Cyst-ene Chapel.

I think it's a good idea to wear two different deodorants, one under each armpit.
But hey, that's just my two scents.

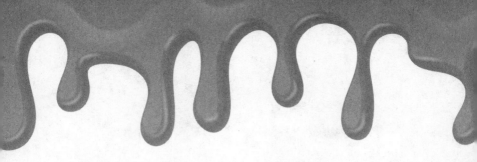

Did you hear about the guy whose dentist diagnosed him with bad breath?
He told him to either stop scratching his butt or biting his fingernails.

What do body odor and peaches have in common?
They both grow around pits.

Is it okay to bite your toenails?
It's a stretch, but okay.

What's the toughest playground game?
Skin tag!

What sounds like onions but doesn't taste like onions?
Bunions.

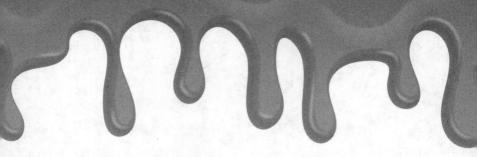

What's worse than getting skin tags?
When your skin tags catch on a fence.

What's the color of strawberries but doesn't taste like strawberries?
A scar.

Another book to read:
A World of Flakes, *by Dan D. Ruff.*

How did all
this dandruff
wind up on
my sweater?
It's a real
head scratcher.

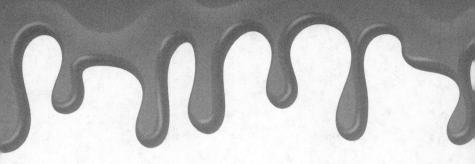

What should you do if someone rolls their eyes at you?
Pick them up and roll them right back.

What's the difference between a grilled cheese sandwich and a cyst?
The sandwich doesn't ooze as much when you bite into it.

How do you make yourself appealing?
Skip the sunscreen and get a sunburn. You'll be a peeling for days.

Kid #1: How do you know when it's time to clean your ears?
Kid #2: Huh?

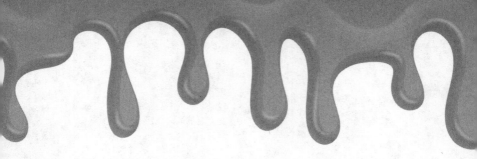

Mom: Stop biting your nails.
Kid: Hey, it's normal.
Mom: Not when they're sharp and rusty and in an old barn wall!

Why did the kid not mind the burrowing parasites?
They had just gotten under his skin.

What do you call lice on a bald guy? Lost.

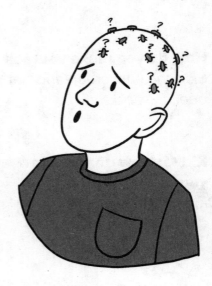

Who lives in your house and is covered in pustules?
Your cyst-er.

I got a new stick of deodorant today. The instructions said "remove cap and push up bottom." I don't know how that's supposed to help.

Some people criticize my dandruff.
I just brush it off.

7

THOSE DISGUSTING ANIMALS

Why do lap dogs have the
worst smelling poop?
Because they're so spoiled.

What's yellow, sticky, and smells like bananas?
Monkey snot.

What did one fly say to the other fly?"
"Excuse me, is this stool taken?"

What do you call a monkey that farts in church?
A badboon.

Did you hear about the lion with diarrhea?
It was a cat-astrophe.

What's another name for elephant poop?
Peanut butter.

What's wet, orange, and smells like peanuts?
Elephant puke.

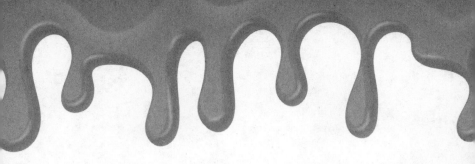

How can you tell the difference between rhino and elephant poop?
Elephants work for peanuts.

Why did the fleas leave the dirty, disgusting kid alone?
The lice had already called dibs.

What does a dog call a litter box?
A buffet.

What would you find in a cow's nose?
Moo-cus.

How can you tell if there's a monkey in your fridge?
Hair in the butter.

What do you get when you freeze the litter box?
Poop-cicles.

**Did you hear about the joke about
squirrel poop?**
It's nutty!

What kind of dog has the most germs?
A bac-terrier.

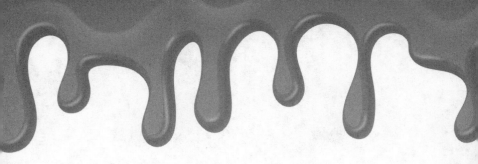

Why did the chicken cross the road?
To get to the bathroom as quickly as possible.

What's invisible and smells like bananas?
Monkey farts.

Why do tapeworms make good detectives?
They know how to get to the bottom of things.

Where does a duck rub toilet paper?
On its quack.

A bear and a rabbit are pooping in the woods. The bear asked the rabbit," "Do you have problems with poop sticking to your fur? The rabbit replied, "No." "That's great!" said the bear as he grabbed the rabbit and started wiping.

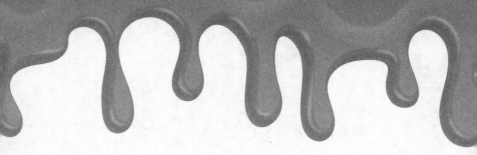

What's another name for cow poop?
Beef patties.

What does pig poop smell like?
It stoinks!

What do dogs call vomit?
Second dinner.

How do you make a pig fly?
Feed it a bowl of beans.

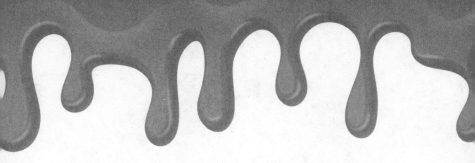

What smells like ham and poop?
Pig farts.

What do a diaper and a tired dog have in common?
Heavy pants.

What's red, chunky, and smells like a gazelle?
Cheetah puke.

What gets better with age?
Dog poop.

What do dogs call it when they poop in their crate?
A midnight snack.

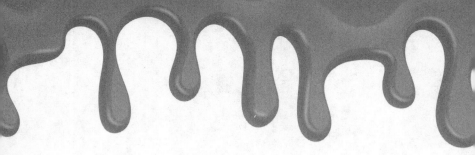

What are grizzly bear farts like?
Silent but violent.

Why do horses fart when they gallop?
That's how they get up to full horsepower.

Why didn't the pig laugh at the loud fart?
Because he was a boar.

Why is alligator
pee so yellow?
They drink
a lot of
Gator-ade.

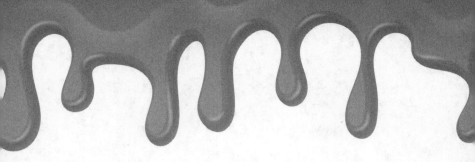

What do cows pee?
Cheese Whiz.

What's invisible and smells like vegetables?
Bunny farts.

Why did the cheetah eat the gazelle?
He was in the mood for some fast food.

What is a fly's favorite dessert?
Cow pie.

What kind of dinosaur can't stop urinating?
A pee-rex.

What did the skunk say to the farting man?
"Don't make such a stink. I've got you covered."

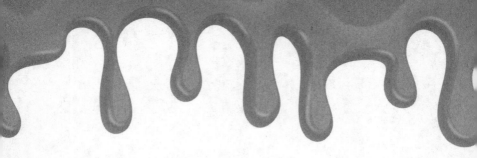

How did the skunk feel after being run over by a car?
Smelly and tired.

Two kids were walking down the street. They came across a pile of dog poop. "Is that dog poop?" one asked. "It smells like dog poop," said the other. Then they both put their fingers in it, and one said, "Feels like dog poop." The other one replied, "Good thing we didn't step in it!"

What should you do if pigs start to fly?
Grab an umbrella.

Two bats hang upside-down in a cave. The first bat asked the second, "Do you remember the worst day of your life?" The second bat replied, "Yeah. The day I had diarrhea!"

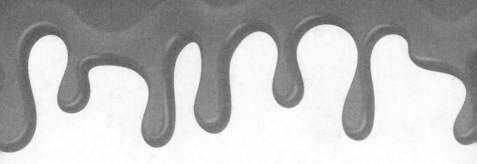

A bird in the hand...
...will probably poop in your hand.

Did you hear about the turkey with a farting problem?
It shot stuffing all the way across the dinner table.

What animal always throws up after it eats?
A yak.

What's thick, slimy, and hangs from tall trees?
Giraffe snot.

Why did the spider fall into the toilet bowl?
It got peed off.

What do you give a giraffe with diarrhea?
Lots of space.

What's furry, loves to kiss,
and loves to drink toilet water?
A dog.

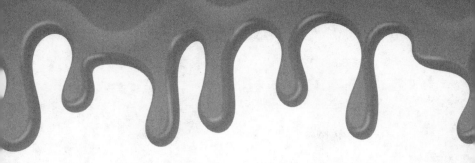

What does a dog call its thrown-up breakfast?
Lunch.

How do you keep flies out of the kitchen?
Leave a bunch of dog poop in the living room.

What do you call a dog with no legs?
Whatever you want; they're not coming.

How do you make ground beef?
Remove the cow's legs.

Why did the monkey fall out of the tree?
Because it was dead.

How do you do an impression of a bird?
Eat a couple of worms.

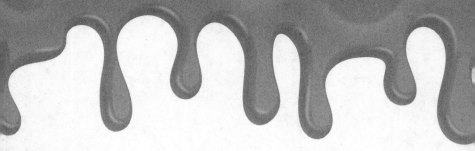

Knock-knock! *Who's there?*
Rhino. *Rhino who?*
Rhino you're the one that farted.

Did you hear about the platypus with diarrhea?
Now he's a splatypus.

Knock-knock! *Who's there?*
Termite. *Termite who?*
Termites the night I can finally poo, thanks to these laxatives!

What did Godzilla make after he ate Tokyo?
A city dump.

What happens if the dog doesn't eat his breakfast on Monday morning?
Mom makes meatloaf for dinner Monday night.

How do you tell which end of a worm is which?
Place it in a bowl of flour and watch to see which side farts.

Did you hear the giant had a nosebleed?
It's all over town.

What do bunnies poop? Easter eggs.

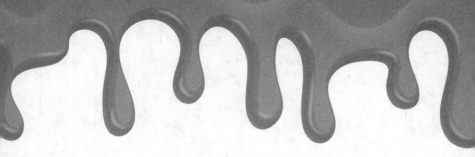

What's green and chunky and smells like zebras?
Lion vomit.

What do you call a bean-eating cat?
Puss 'n' Toots.

Why did the chicken cross the road?
The other chicken farted.

Did you hear about the skunk who lost its glasses?
It fell in love with a fart.

What is a snail?
A booger wearing a helmet.

What does an elephant keep in its trunk?
A gallon of snot.

What's the difference between a cookie and a slug?
The slug breaks down when you dip it in milk.

Customer: Waiter, there's a roach in my soup.
Waiter: Well keep it down, we don't have enough to go around.

Customer: Waiter, there's a roach in my soup.
Waiter: And it's on the house!

What did the banana say to the maggot?
"You're boring me!"

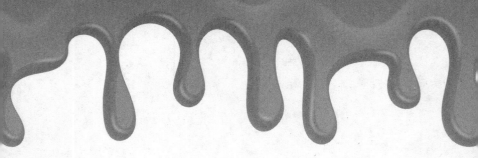

What's the difference between roaches and maggots?
Maggots have a creamy center.

Why do maggots like wounds?
They don't have to fight over the scab.

How do you make sure your dog gets fleas?
Start from scratch.

Patient: There are leeches all over my back!
Doctor: Eh, they don't drink much.

Kid: Do slugs taste good?
Dad: Why?
Kid: There's one on your fork. Or it was before you took that big bite.

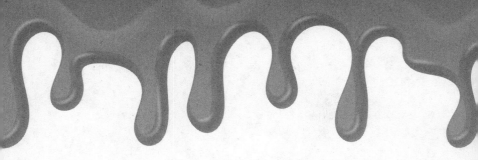

Why do dogs eat vomit?
So the other dogs don't.

How are roaches like raisins?
Both show up in your cereal.

Why don't fleas get cold?
They're always inside of fur.

What do you
call a deer
without
any eyes?
No-eye deer!

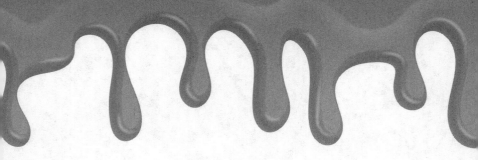

Kid #1: Is your dog potty trained?
Kid #2: Yep.
Dog poops.
Kid #1: I thought you said your dog was potty trained.
Kid #2: That's not my dog.

What has 50 legs and can't walk very well?
Half of a centipede.

Scientists have discovered a creature that licks itself, eats the waste of other animals, and might already be living in your home.
It's called a "dog."

What do you call a bear who loves honey, doesn't wear pants, and smells?
Winnie the Pew.

Who's in charge of your head lice?
The head louse

Why do dogs poop outside?
Because they can.

Did you hear the cat was fined?
For littering.

How did the poop cross the road?
It was still hanging out of the dog's rear end.

How do you stop getting sick from insect bites?
Stop biting those insects.

What has four legs and flies?
A dead cow.

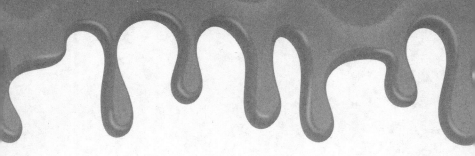

How can pterodactyls use the bathroom so quietly?
Their P is silent.

How do you make a mouse drink?
Put it in a blender.

Why do giraffes have long necks? Because their feet stink.

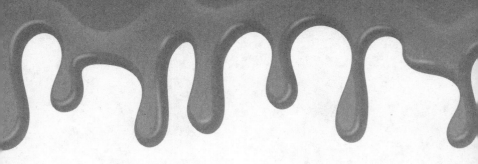

What did the chef do to the daddy longlegs she found in the meatloaf?
She turned it into a daddy shortlegs.

A teenager was dating a girl for a long time when he was going to meet her parents. The man had a burrito that afternoon, so he was feeling flatulent. He let a loud one out on the couch, and his girlfriend's mother said "Spot." "Oh good, she blamed it on the dog," the guy thought. So he let another one come out. "Spot. Come here." He let one more out, and then the mother yelled, "Spot, come over here before he poops on you, too!"

What's black and white and red all over?
An exploding zebra.

What's black and white and red all over?
A constipated zebra.

Customer: Waiter, there's a fly in my soup.
Waiter: Don't worry, it probably died in the microwave.

What goes "cluck, cluck, bang!"?
An exploding chicken.

Never, ever let a chicken use your bathroom. They always leave a fowl smell.

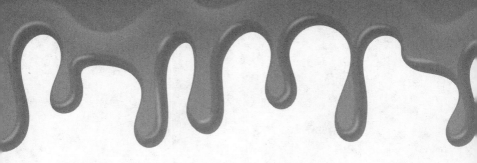

Why did the guy put corn in his shoes?
For his pigeon toes.

Customer: Why is there a fly in my soup?
Waiter: We ran out of spiders.

What happened when the cow grazed in a field of mint?
It made peppermint patties.

What do you call a bag full of used-up lab monkeys?
Rhesus pieces.

Why are dogs good at telling time?
They're covered in ticks.

What should you do if an elephant eats you?
Run around until you're pooped.

What's the difference between head lice and nits?
The nits are much crunchier.

"There's a blood-sucking insect in my French cheese," said Conner briefly.

Customer: Waiter, what's this fly doing on my meal?
Waiter: By the looks of it, laying eggs.

Knock-knock! *Who's there?*
Howard. *Howard who?*
Howard I know the dog would puke up the cat poop he ate?

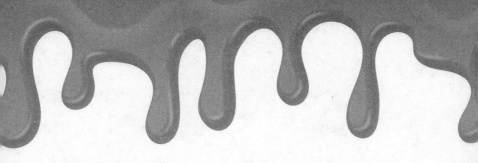

What's fluffy, white, and covered in brown goo?
A poodle that threw up all over itself.

Do you know what the white stuff in bird poop is?
That's bird poop, too.

How did the T. rex feel
after vomiting all night?
Dino-sore.

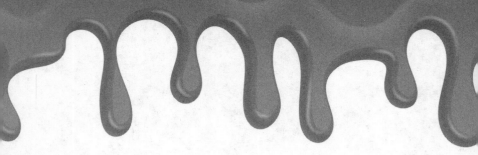

What's another name for cat poop?
Turrrrrrrds.

What's another name for panda poop?
Endangered feces.

What do you give an elephant with diarrhea?
Room!

Why was there poop in the middle of the road?
That's where the chicken left it.

What can you do with a bunch of turtle poop?
Make it into turtle-izer.

I got a job cleaning horse manure.
Well, the ad promised a stable income.

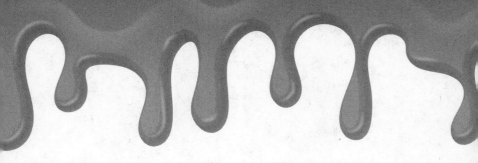

What happened to the boy who sat under a cow?
He got a pat on the head.

They say that the dinosaurs farted themselves to death.
It was an ex-stink-tion level event.

Why doesn't Batman like visitors to the Batcave?
He's embarrassed by all the guano.

Where do cows fart from?
Their dairy-airs.

What makes other dinosaurs run faster and farther than a T. rex roar?
A T. rex fart.

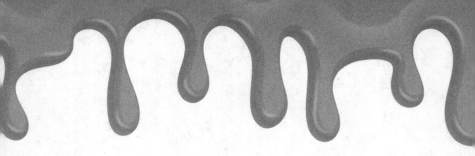

What happens when you run out of manure on a farm?
You have to make doo.

Why did the first fish grow legs and head up onto shore?
It was looking for a bathroom.

If H2O is inside a fire hydrant, what's on the outside?
K9P.

Which cows are the scariest?
The ones who wear leather jackets and order steak.

What's the difference between a beetle and spaghetti?
A beetle will stay on your fork.

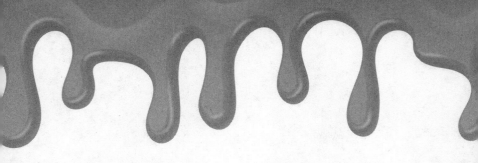

Kid #1: What's red, black, and has big sharp teeth?
Kid #2: What?
Kid #1: I don't know either, but it just crawled into your ear.

My friend and I formed a comedy duo.
We do animal impressions—she makes the sounds, and I do the smells.

Never stand too close to a duck.
Their breath is fowl.

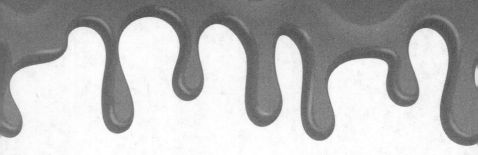

Kid #1: A bird pooped on me the other day but I was thankful.
Kid #2: Why?
Kid #1: For the fact that cows don't fly.

Knock-knock! *Who's there?*
Amal. *Amal who?*
Amal covered in bird poop!

Why do gnats hate to throw up?
It attracts flies.

Why do mama birds vomit into their babies' mouths?
It's good to start the day with a hot breakfast.

What does a puking dog say?
"B'arf!"

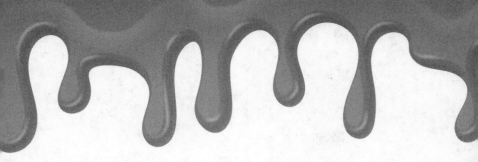

What do you call a dog with diarrhea?
A poo-dle.

What's the difference between fresh dog poop and school lunch?
The dog poop is warm.

What's stinky and shaped like a foot?
Stepped-in dog poop.

Where do sheep do their business? In the baaa-throom.

EDIBLE
DERANGEMENTS

Which veggie
would you
find in
a toilet?
A leek.

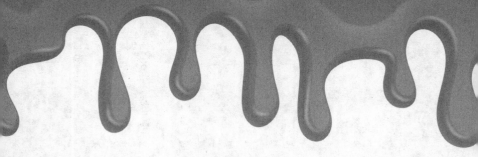

Why did the baker rub dough all over his feet?
To make cornbread.

That chocolate cake was so good I sunk my teeth into it.
I'm sorry if you find any when you have your slice.

Dad: The doctor asked me to freeze a stool sample.
Kid: Oh, so that's why those chocolate popsicles tasted so gross.

What's the grossest tasting bean?
Dung beans.

How can you turn rotten eggs into vomit?
Eat them and wait.

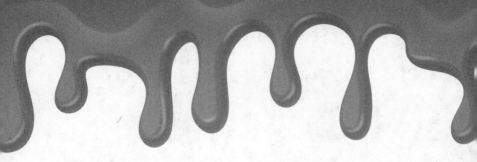

The lunch in my school cafeteria is so bad.
The flies and rats transferred to another school.

The cannibal didn't like his friends.
So he just ate a stranger instead.

How do you ruin a peanut butter sandwich?
With toe jam.

Why do cannibals like to eat brains?
Food for thought!

Why don't zombies eat comedians?
They taste funny.

Why don't cannibals eat organs?
They're hard to stomach.

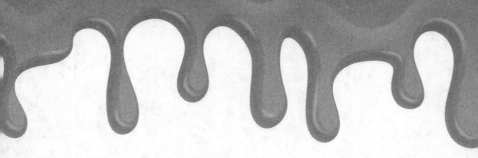

Patient: Help me doctor, I have an almond stuck in one nostril and a pecan in the other.
Doctor: That's nuts.

Why don't cannibals like crematoriums?
They burn all the food.

How do cannibals freshen their breath?
With Men Toes.

What's the difference between a toilet brush and a cookie? You can't dip a toilet brush in your milk.

What's sweet on the outside and green on the inside?
A snot-filled doughnut.

Why did the coffee smell like dirt?
It was just ground.

What do you get when you feed rice cereal to a baby?
Snap crackle poop!

What's green and lumpy and comes in small containers?
Spoiled yogurt.

Mom: We're having grandma for dinner tonight!
Kid: Can't we just have pizza?

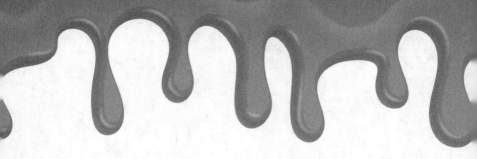

Stranger: Why's your son crying?
Parent: He has a corn dog stuck up his nose.
Stranger: Why is your daughter crying?
Parent: Her brother stole her lunch.

What's red and green and shakes?
Rotten meat gelatin.

What does a cannibal call
a person in a hammock?
Breakfast in bed.

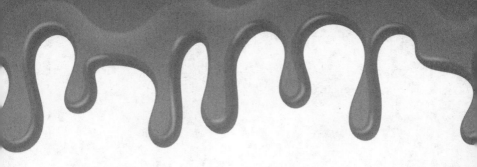

I prefer smooth peanut butter to the crunchy stuff.
That way you can't taste all the bugs from the factory that died in there.

I saw a witch picking at her feet.
Which I guess is where candy corn comes from.

How are roaches different from raisins?
Roaches are a lot crunchier.

"I just love that shake cheese you put on the pizza," the customer said. "We don't have that here," the cook said, scratching his head.

What's cold, green, and has a cherry on top?
A snot sundae.

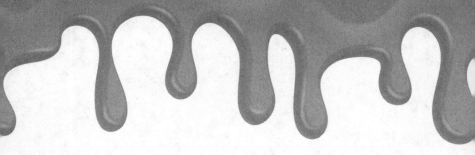

What's green and white and comes in a quart-size plastic container?
Year-old cottage cheese.

What's white on the outside, black on the inside, and wiggles?
A roach sandwich.

What's creamy, brown, and dangerous?
Pudding filled with venomous snakes.

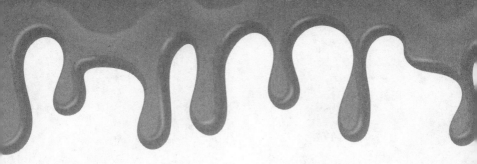

What's made of vomit, potatoes, carrots, and meat?
Beef spew.

Why don't cannibals attack hospitals?
They hate how the stitches get caught in their teeth.

How can you tell someone wearing tight pants ate chili?
Their ankles swell up when they fart.

How do you make tear gas?
Mix onions and beans.

What fruit tastes horrible and is found inside of a banana peel?
A poonana.

"Thanks so much for bringing me that fruit with all the fiber in it," said Erin applaudingly.

Kid: These hot dogs smell like farts!
Dad: That's because they're frankfarters!

What breakfast cereal tastes the worst?
Poop Loops

Which breakfast cereal smells the worst? Toot Loops.

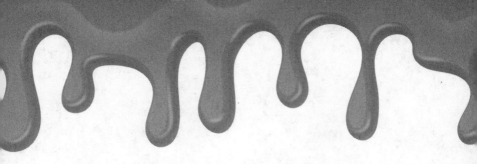

It's not red meat that's bad for you.
Fuzzy green meat is what will really make you sick.

Should you eat potato chips with your fingers?
No, your fingers would taste terrible! And it would hurt to bite through them.

Kid #1: That kid over there smells exactly like fish.
Kid #2: That poor sole.

Did you hear about the butcher who backed into a meat grinder?
He got a little behind in his work.

What do you get when you eat peanut butter and baked beans?
A fart that sticks to the roof of your butt.

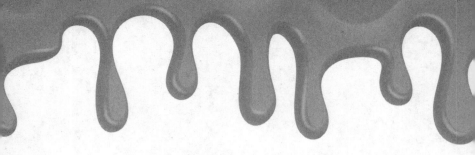

I pee on the side of the bowl to make less noise.
Still, my mom wasn't too happy about me ruining her cereal.

How do you make a turd float?
Put it in a glass of root beer.

Kid: What are you doing with that manure?
Farmer: Putting it on these strawberries.
Kid: At my house we usually use powdered sugar.

How do you
make pickles?
Shove a
cucumber up
your nose.

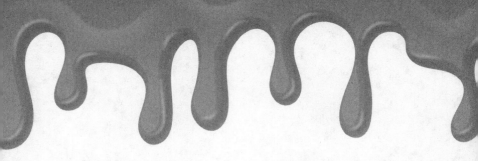

How can you tell if there are spider pieces in your cookies?
Read the ingredients list.

What should you never have for breakfast?
A big glass of orange deuce.

The zombie had never eaten out of a skull before.
But they liked to keep an open mind.

What's green, slimy, and tastes like spinach farts?
Spinach!

What's great about a birthday cake made of beans?
It can blow itself out.

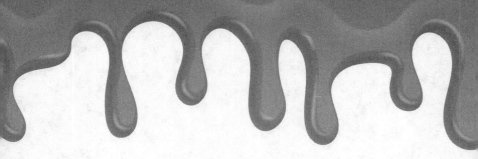

Kid: Why can't we just throw things away in a garbage can like everyone else?
Parent: Don't talk with your mouth full!

The bottom fell out of my world.
So I started eating prunes, and the world fell out of my bottom.

Why did the burglar eat cement?
He was a hardened criminal.

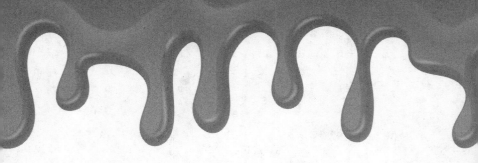

What's brown, squishy, and hairy?
A grilled cheese sandwich you dropped on the carpet last week.

What's the difference between chocolate and poop?
If you don't know, never buy me chocolate.

What kind of peas are brown?
Poo-peas.

What do cannibals do at weddings?
They toast the couple.

"And here's your portion," said the cannibal half-heartedly.

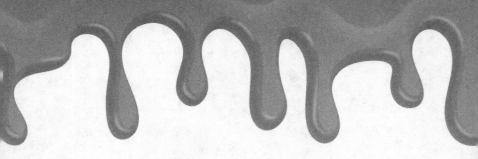

The cannibal got expelled from school.
He kept trying to butter up the teacher.

The doctor said if I'm feeling sick I should have a hot bath.
But I could only drink about a cup or two.

Why did the cannibal eat
the tightrope walker?
He was after a balanced diet.

I put two slices of bread all over my legs and feet. That's how you make a below-knee sandwich.

Don't go to that new cannibal restaurant.
It costs an arm and a leg.

What kind of chips do you get if you run corn through your feet?
Dori-Toes.

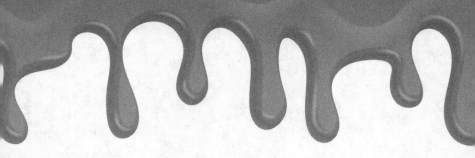

What do you call fish you put in your shoes and walked around on all day?
Shoe-shi.

Why did the cannibal tutor quit her job?
She didn't think it was worth it for only two pupils.

Why did the vampire eat his dog?
He loves pupperoni.

Kid #1: The food in our school cafeteria is great.
Kid #2: If you're an insect.

When do zombies come out to feed?
During a brainstorm.

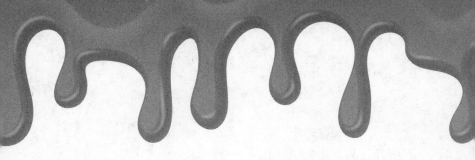

What should you never order in a French restaurant?
Poofflé.

How do
you make
steamed buns?
Pour hot
water down
your pants.

Why did the kid eat the three dollars his parents gave him? It was his lunch money.

Why did the cannibal become a detective?
To grill the suspects.

Why should you never sneeze on your friend's school lunch?
It might make it taste better, and then you'll have to sneeze on their lunch every day.

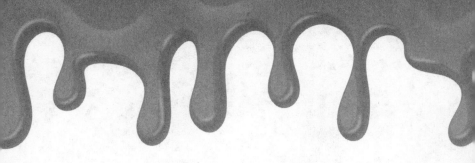

Man: Doctor! I have a piece of lettuce peeking out of my butt!
Doctor: *Well, this is just the tip of the iceberg.*

What grows in the ground, smells like a bathroom, and can be made into French fries?
Poo-tatoes.

What's white and slimy and comes out of your nose?
Milk, if it's a good joke.

What's cool,
white, and has
a bottom
at the top?
A toilet.

What's the worst part about using an office bathroom?
The paperwork.

Why did the man leave the public bathroom?
He'd turd enough from the stall next to him.

Don't be afraid of a brand-new pair of underwear.
It's merely unfarted territory.

Why is toilet paper so direct? It gets to the bottom of things.

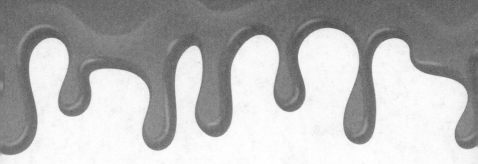

Knock-knock! *Who's there?*
Abbott. *Abbott who?*
Abbott time we got a candle for this bathroom!

My window looks out directly into my neighbor's bathroom.
It's a room with an ewww.

What stinks and flies through the air at 500 miles per hour?
An airplane bathroom.

Knock-knock! *Who's there?*
Gas. *Gas who?*
Gas who stunk up the bathroom!?

What do you call a bathroom in Finland?
Helstinki.

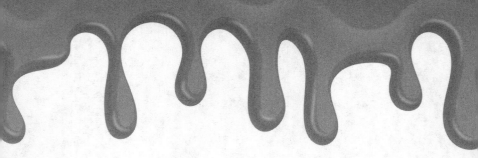

A gross man went to a doctor and was told he needed a urine and a feces sample.
He handed the doctor his underwear.

Patient: Doctor! I need your help. When I eat chicken, chicken comes out of my bottom, and when I eat carrots, it comes out of my bottom too!
Doctor: Just eat poop.

Why do golfers wear two pairs of underwear? In case they get a hole in one.

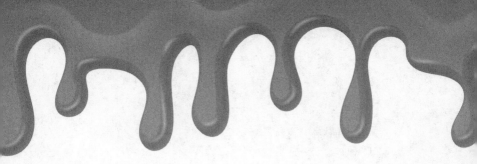

Knock-knock! *Who's there?*
Watt. *Watt who?*
Watt died in here?

What's tight, white, and full of holes?
Dad's underwear.

Dad: Why are you wearing your underwear on the outside of your pants?
Son: To keep them clean!

When is TP ever a bad thing?
When you don't use enough.

Knock-knock! *Who's there?*
Arthur. *Arthur who?*
Arthur any plumbers on duty? Because we're gonna need one!

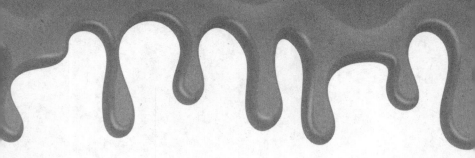

What should a plumber never bring to a potluck?
Chili.

What's the first thing they teach at plumbing school?
Don't lick your fingers.

Kid #1: You know your underwear must be strong.
Kid #2: How's that?
Kid #1: If it can stay intact with your farts.

What kind of salad would you find in a pair of underwear?
Wedge.

In putting on your underwear each day, remember:
Yellow in front, brown in back.

What do you call underwear full of farts?
Thunderwear.

The best underwear jokes are brief.

How do they put the leg holes in underwear?
They give them to a guy who farts the holes through.

What does
a pirate keep
in their
underwear?
Booty.

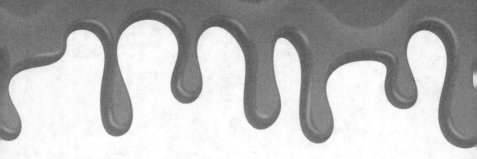

Knock-knock! *Who's there?*
Sausage. *Sausage who?*
Sausage a mess you left in that bathroom.

I love putting on warm underwear fresh out of the dryer.
Even though I got kicked out of the laundromat.

How are zebras like your dad's underwear?
The stripes.

What underwear smells like farts?
Toot of the Loom!

Knock-knock! *Who's there?*
Donna. *Donna who?*
Donna forget to flush when you're done in there!

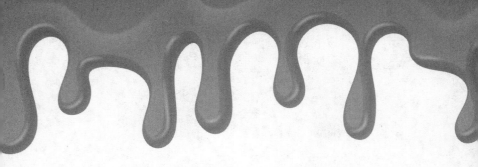

Did you hear the joke about the toilet?
It's pretty filthy!

Can you name two reasons not to drink from a toilet?
Number one and number two.

"My underpants are too small," said Isaac, briefly.

What did the monster do after it used the bathroom? It lit a monster match.

"I finished cleaning out the septic tank," David said successfully.

"While this over here is a toilet seat," Maya went on.

"I shouldn't have waited so long to clean the toilet," Pearl said crustily.

"The bulb burst in the bathroom, and I couldn't see what I was doing," Gordon said delightedly.

"Better get some air circulating in here fast, it stinks!" Carl said fanatically.

"Don't you have anything to get rid of the smell in here?" Johnny asked, incensed.

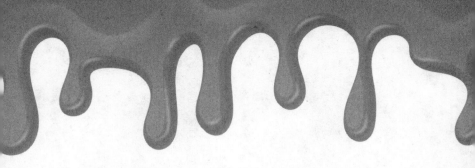

"There's a free portable toilet over here," Nancy admitted.

"You've stowed his ashes commendably," was Matt's well-earned compliment.

Knock-knock! *Who's there?*
Figs. *Figs who?*
Figs the toilet! You're the one who clogged it.

"I installed the new toilet!" Alexis said, flushed with success.

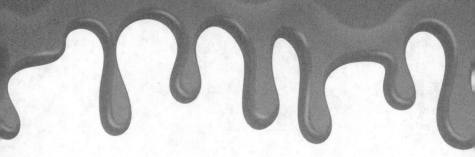

Why did the plumber pee on his shoes?
So he could work from home.

Want to hear a joke about germs?
It's going around.

If your underwear smells so bad they knock people out, they're stun-dies.

Why don't racehorses wear underwear?
Because it rides up on them!

As the plumber reached into his tool belt to unclog a toilet and pulled out a big spoon, he realized he'd left his plunger in the pot at home.

They seemed like normal underwear until they exploded.
I guess I bought Fruit of the Boom.

Knock-knock! *Who's there?*
Bernie. *Bernie who?*
Bernie candle or something!

I only use public restrooms that have been officially vetted by critics.
They're peer reviewed.

Never take a Pokémon into the bathroom with you.
They may Pikachu.

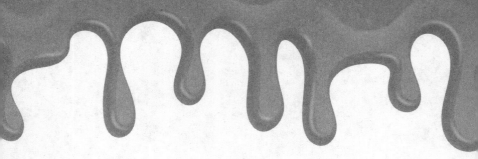

Knock-knock! *Who's there?*
Dawn. *Dawn who?*
Dawn sit down there without wiping it the seat first!

Knock-knock! *Who's there?*
Distinct. *Distinct who?*
Distinct when you come out of the bathroom is disgusting.

Why do writers spend so much time in the bathroom? They're in there writing poo-ems.

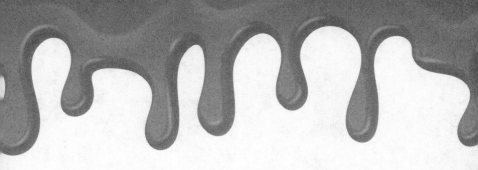

Did you hear about the man who only bathed on his birthday?
No, but you could probably smell him from there.

Doctor: How have your bowel movements been?
Patient: Not great. The toilet's been broken, so I don't go as much, and things are really painful down there.
Doctor: Have you tried taking the plunger out first?

What did the plumber say right before he got sick?
"One little taste couldn't hurt!"

What should you do if you're worried about running out of toilet paper?
Make sure you have plenty of washcloths.

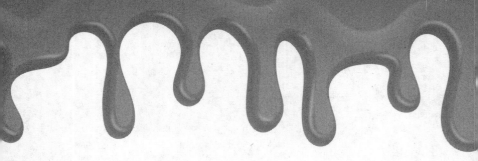

What happened when all the loggers used the bathroom at the same time?
A logjam.

Never tell a toilet your secrets.
It leaks.

Kid: Can I lick the bowl?
Mom: No, just flush it!

What are
relief maps
for?
Finding the
bathroom.

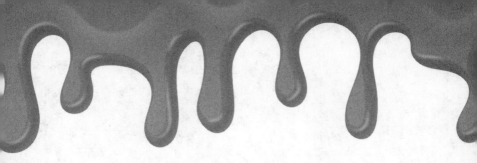

Knock-knock! *Who's there?*
Fink. *Fink who?*
Fink you can flush next time?

I wondered why the toilet paper was so itchy.
Until I realized it was scratch paper.

Did you hear about the thieves who took all of the toilets from the police station?
The detectives had nothing to go on.

What's the most common toilet serial number?
"4U2PN."

How are toilet bowls like wedding anniversaries?
Grown-ups tend to miss them both.

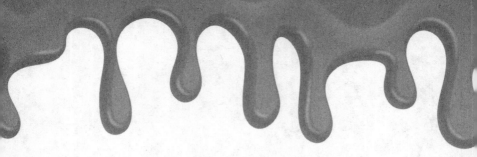

What smells twice as bad as a toilet?
Two toilets.

What do you call a toilet on wheels?
A dump truck.

Check out this book:
A History of Plumbers' Pants, *by Sawyer Crack.*

What can you say about someone who refuses to stop pooping in their pants?
An undeterred undie-turd.

Husband: I should pee before we get on the plane.
Wife: Yes. And I should pee myself.
Husband: Or you could just use the bathroom over there.

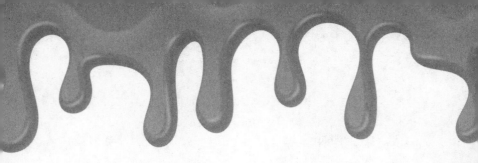

Knock-knock! *Who's there?*
Unaware. *Unaware who?*
Unaware is what you put on first!

What's the difference between a sink and a toilet?
If you don't know, I wouldn't want to visit your house.

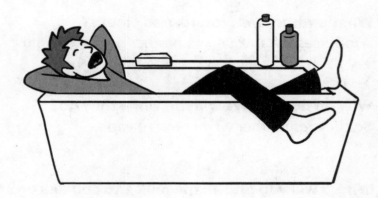

Why do people fall asleep in the bathroom?
Because it's also called a restroom.

Knock-knock! *Who's there?*
Lou. *Lou who?*
Lou is free if you need it.

How come there's a hole in the toilet seat?
Would you want to use one that didn't have a hole in it?

What's white, wet, round, and smells?
A toilet seat after your little brother gets done with it.

Why do dumb guys whistle while they go?
So they remember which end to wipe.

Where will you find all the milk and cookies on Christmas morning?
In Santa's toilet.

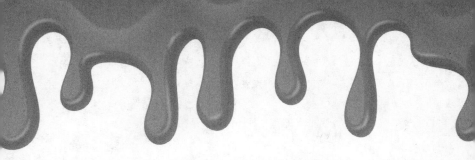

Why do underpants make good detectives?
Because they're so good at going undercover.

What's covered in 500 million people who can't control their bowels?
The incontinent of North America.

What's the most fun thing about white toilet paper?
You get to color it in yourself!

Why wasn't the toilet ready for use? It was still potty training.

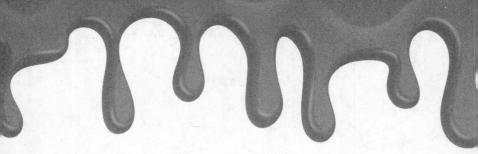

Patient: I'm not feeling well.
Doctor: I noticed you put a piece of pizza in your underpants.
Patient: So?
Doctor: Clearly, you're not eating right.

What do composers do after they die?
Decompose.

Why are there no bathrooms in some banks?
Because not all banks accept deposits.

What's a mortician's favorite game?
Tag!

How do you know the bathroom floor is too dirty?
When the slugs leave a trail that says "wash me."

How did the dentist become a surgeon?
When his hand slipped while drilling a tooth.

My grandma always said that the way to someone's heart was through their stomach.
She was a terrible heart surgeon.

Why did the kid fall asleep on the toilet? He'd taken a relaxative.

ABOUT THE AUTHOR

BRIAN BOONE is the author of *The Jokiest Joking Joke Book Ever Written . . . No Joke!* and many other books about everything from inventions to paper airplanes to magic to TV. He's written jokes for lots of funny websites and he lives in Oregon with his family.

ABOUT THE ILLUSTRATOR

AMANDA BRACK has a passion for drawing and illustration, and enjoys the creativity of working on a wide variety of projects in her freelance career. She lives in Queens, New York.